BREAKING THE GENDER BARRIER
IN YOUTH MINISTRY

Mark –
Keep going for it!!
Diane Elliot

BREAKING THE GENDER BARRIER

IN YOUTH MINISTRY

Edited by

Diane Elliot & Ginny Olson

VICTOR BOOKS

A DIVISION OF SCRIPTURE PRESS PUBLICATIONS INC.
USA CANADA ENGLAND

Editors: Afton Rorvik, Sarah M. Peterson
Designer: Grace K. Chan Mallette

Library of Congress Cataloging-in-Publication Data

Breaking the gender barrier in youth ministry / edited by Diane Elliot and Ginny Olson.
    p.   cm.
    ISBN 1-56476-497-4
    1. Church work with youth.   2. Sex role — Religious aspects — Christianity.   3. Evangelicalism — United States. I. Elliot, Diane. II. Olson, Ginny.
BV4447.B698 1995
259'.23 — dc20   95-35482
                                                  CIP

---

1 2 3 4 5 6 7 8 9 10 Printing / Year 99 98 97 96 95

VICTOR BOOKS
A division of SP Publications, Inc.
Wheaton, Illinois 60187

Contents

Foreword: Becky Tirabassi 11
Introduction: Diane Elliot and Ginny Olson 13

ONE / Beyond Kitchens and Kool-Aid
19 *A theological look at women in youth ministry*
Helen Musick and Karen Thomas

TWO / Maximizing Our Differences
33 *How a woman ministers differently than a man*
Kara Eckmann

**THREE / Ministry Would Be Great If It
Weren't for the People**
52 *Effective team ministry*
Laurie Polich

FOUR / Dynamic Duos
59 *Partnerships that work*
Mike DeVito and Kara Eckmann

FIVE / Choose Your Own Adventure
72 *Women in various seasons of ministry*
Kara Eckmann with Eilleen Rollerson, Lisa Walker, and Nancy Wilson

SIX / Search for the Right Fit
88 *Finding out who you are and how you minister*
Rick Dunn and Jana Sundene

SEVEN / Barriers along the Way
103 *Understanding and overcoming the obstacles
women face*
Ginny Olson

EIGHT / You're Not Alone
115 *The benefits of effective networking*
Diane Elliot

NINE / What Men Can Do to Help
129 *One man's journey toward awareness*
Tim McLaughlin

TEN / Men Influencing Female Students
138 *Healthy relationships with young women*
Jim Burns

ELEVEN / **Thinking Creatively**
146   *Programming ideas for women ministering to girls*
Karen Grant

TWELVE / **Helping Girls Who Hurt**
159   *Intervention for girls in crisis*
Saundra Hensel with Terryl Overpeck, MA, LMST

THIRTEEN / **When Bandages Aren't Enough**
174   *Addressing the sexual issues of girls*
Nancy Sanders

FOURTEEN / **Cross-Gender Counseling**
183   *Guidelines for ministry effectiveness*
Steve Gerali, D.Phil. and Janice Gerali, RN

FIFTEEN / **Finishing Well**
197   *Equipped for the journey*
Lynn Ziegenfuss

NOTES /
211

APPENDIX / **Resources for Effective Ministry**
215   **Compiled by Jean Tippit**

Acknowledgments

My life's journey has brought me in contact with some remark-
able people who have significantly impacted my life. These are
the women who stepped out on a limb to do what had never
been done before. Women who poured their hearts and souls
into students, then turned around and encouraged others to do
the same. Women who refused to be paralyzed by the word *impossible* because they have done the impossible, and more, time
and again. Women who fearlessly blazed a trail, making it a little
easier for others to follow. Women who have made my journey
in youth ministry a whole lot more bearable, fun, and exciting.
To all of you, my friends, colleagues, and colaborers, I thank
you. There is Ginny Olson, my cofounder, fearless visionary, and
favorite coffee buddy; Saundra Hensel, who joined us shortly after we began our journey and helped to lighten the load; Beryl
Glass, who always makes us look good even when we don't deserve it; Kara Eckmann, our West coast connection who adds
some California diversity to our Midwest mentality; Jana
Sundene, who brought the credentials that made us respect-
able; Jean DeVaty, the "new girl," who adds balance and fun
(who really isn't new anymore but will always carry the title); my
two pseudo-daughters Beth Gray and Val Byrnes who faithfully
did whatever needed doing to make this book a reality; and to
all the contributing authors that gave so much of themselves.
Thanks, team, for your faith, creativity, endurance, example,
and friendship. You are truly an awesome team.

A special thanks to Liz Duckworth and Victor Books who
had faith in us even when no one else would take the risk. Thank
you for believing!

To *all* my family (which will remain nameless since it
would take most of the book to list all of your names . . . you
know who you are): your security, love, example, and encouragement have made me who I am. To my sweet, furry boys,

Stormy and Pepper, your desires for the simple pleasures in life have kept me sane in an otherwise crazy world. And last, but not least, to the wonderful man who gave us his undying support and kept us supplied with chocolate while surrendering the house, his office, and often his finances to a group of impetuous women — my husband David. Thanks hon. Your faith in God, me, and the Journey team is an inspiration.

— Diane Elliot

There have been many pilgrims — both men and women — along the way who have greatly helped me in my journey in youth ministry and, thus, this project. In particular, I couldn't have asked for better partners than the Journey team itself — Saundra, Jana, Kara, and Jean. Their enthusiasm for seeing women in youth ministry has kept the dream alive. Of course, there's the leader of this odd band of sojourners, Diane Elliot — my coeditor, cofounder, and covisionary — the one who helped turn my passion for increasing the possibilities for women in youth ministry into something productive. A longtime fellow pilgrim has been my roommate Terryl, who has logged many youth ministry miles with me and has been a guide, supporter, and the dearest soul friend one could ask for. And Randy, Chris, and Andy, who have patiently helped me to process both the internal and external barriers that I've faced and somehow make sense of it all. Most of all, I'm grateful for my parents, who taught me that no barrier should stand in the way of what I feel God is calling me to do. Thanks for encouraging me to dream.

— Ginny Olson

Dedication

In memory of a very special lady, Barb Wiegele, we would like to dedicate this book to all the female volunteer youth workers who are on the front lines of student ministries.

Still a teen herself, Barb began working with junior highers in 1980 at Willow Creek Community Church in South Barrington, Illinois. She did everything from leading a small group to overseeing and training volunteer leaders to being the program director of the church's junior high summer camp.

It was Barb who introduced us [Ginny Olson and Diane Elliot] to one another. The result was the birth of Journey Publications, an organization dedicated to the leadership development of volunteer and professional women in youth ministry.

In 1992 Barb was featured in the very first Journey *publication. When we interviewed Barb, she was asked why she was still volunteering instead of moving on to a full-time position. She responded: "Staff people are very important, but volunteers are the heart of youth ministry. Without them, the ministry would die. . . . By volunteering, if I can make one junior high person's life easier, I feel that I have done my job."*

Unknown to Journey *readers, just prior to that interview, Barb had been diagnosed with a rare form of cancer. Although the cancer weakened her to the point where she could not be involved in ministry on a regular basis, she was determined to make it to summer camp that year. At 90 pounds, with a bandanna covering the effects of chemotherapy, Barb led programs and fell in love again with a new group of junior high girls and they with her.*

Barb died Saturday, January 9th, 1993. She never had much money, she never finished her college degree, but she had a passion for seeing God work in junior highers' lives and that was evident. At her funeral sat row after row of people whom Barb had impacted.

When asked what advice she would give to other women in youth ministry during that 1992 interview, Barb replied, "Remember that you, as a woman in youth ministry, are important; what you do matters. You may not see the fruit or results in this lifetime, but you will see it in eternity."

Thank you, Barb, for leaving a path for others to follow. May your legacy continue for generations to come.

Foreword

My first "big" speaking engagement was in 1990. It was called "Pitch and Praise" and was held in Canada for 1,000 kids. The previous year's retreat speaker was the well-known Duffy Robbins. No pressure, right!?

After my first talk, a young man came up to me and said what has been said to me many times by young men since: "I didn't want to come, especially because there was a woman speaker, but you were pretty good!"

After the event, which turned out very well, the event committee mailed my "approval rating" to me. I received a 95 percent approval rating, compared to Duffy's 97 percent approval rating the year before. OK. That felt good — and bad. It felt bad because of the pressure to compete with, and compare myself to, other speakers. Especially, when I was usually the only woman in the vicinity! I quickly discovered the obstacles of being a female speaker in youth ministry.

Five years have passed and I still have young men come up to me after a speaking engagement and express their surprise that a woman speaker could be used by God to touch their lives! I still get evaluated and "ranked" in comparison to other communicators. And, most often, I still am one of the only women on the platform during a night or even a whole week of a youth conference.

Though many things haven't changed in five years of speaking to youth, I have. Instead of focusing on what, why, and how a woman is *different* than a man in youth ministry, I have settled into a philosophy of ministry gleaned from my early Christian and para-church ministry days — when it didn't matter if you were a man or a woman. In the 1970s, our local Christian youth organization simply looked for and recruited all the hands and mouths they could find to drive kids, lead small groups, collect money, organize skits, and speak to kids at meetings and events!

Instead of "the men will speak and the women will be support staff" mentality, each of us — men and women — were first tested for our spiritual gifts, then encouraged to develop and *use* them wherever we could. We *all* worked long hours to reach students with the life-changing message that Jesus Christ loves them so much that He died for them, has prepared a place in heaven for them, and has a unique plan for their lives on earth. (Isn't that what ministry *should* be about?)

It was an exciting time in my life. I met my husband, trained volunteers, discipled kids, developed my speaking skills, and eventually ran my own Campus Life Club. During those years, I was constantly encouraged by my boss to develop and hone my spiritual gifts — no holding back!

And over those first years in ministry, it became apparent that speaking to kids was my passion, my gift, and my usefulness to "the body" I was a part of. It was exhilarating — not intimidating — to be an evangelist involved in youth ministry. I was part of a team of men and women who led, loved, and lifted kids.

Although I have struggled as a woman through some competitive and uncomfortable situations (often because of my own temptations and weaknesses), I have set my heart on pursuing my life call.

I would encourage you to do the same!

The pages of this book are designed to inspire, equip, remind, and encourage *you* to develop the dream and call God has on *your* life. I am confident that as you prayerfully consider the words in this book, you will better know your call. Through the lives and messages of the contributing authors, I believe you will be mentored, goaded, and prepared to face the challenges of being a woman in youth ministry.

If you are a man working with women, I believe you will grow in your understanding and appreciation of the women on your team.

Above all, I hope you will be encouraged to pursue the course of ministry God has for you throughout the seasons of your life, no matter what obstacles you might encounter along the journey!

— *Becky Tirabassi*

Introduction

In a large foyer at the "Palace," a former Communist training center in Siberia now turned meeting facility, I stood with a translator waiting for our missions team to arrive for a Bible study. For a few minutes I waited patiently for the team leader to arrive so that he could get the key from the office to unlock our meeting room. My North American patience quickly ran out, however, and I suggested to the translator that he ask the custodian for the key.

"Only the team leader is able to get the key," he replied in flawless English.

Undaunted, I put my mental energies into conquering the problem. I suggested that he tell the custodian I was the leader. (It seemed like a justifiable fib because it didn't seem like a big deal to pick up a key.) As I was mentally complimenting myself on my quick thinking, he burst out laughing. Confused, I asked what was so funny.

"You can't be the leader," he stated emphatically. "*You're* a woman!"

Several times in the last few years I've heard phrases that were strikingly similar.

- "We could never hire a *woman* youth pastor in this church!"

- "Sorry. We aren't having *women* interns this year in the high school ministry. We had some last year but couldn't find positions for them so we decided to cut the women out of the program."

- "I would love to bring a *woman* high school pastor on board. But to be honest, I don't think that the church board is ready for it."

- "Theologically, I don't think that *women* should be high school youth directors, but there's no reason they couldn't volunteer with their husbands if they happen to be in ministry."

Sometimes being a woman in youth ministry can be frustrating!

Five years ago I was introduced to Ginny Olson, another woman in youth ministry. Over countless cups of coffee and Diet Coke we talked about the challenges and opportunities of being women in youth ministry. After comparing our stories, we realized that at different times we both were ready to call it quits. Sometimes it was just too difficult to walk into one more youth leaders' meeting and be the only one in a skirt. However, independently from one another, we realized that our calling was to be faithful to God with the talents and passions He gave us. For us, for now, that means youth ministry.

After finding out about other women who struggled with similar issues, we decided to start an organization for volunteer and professional women in youth ministry called Journey. We started with a small newsletter that provided a source of encouragement and support for women in their calling. After a short time, several other key individuals, both women and men, affirmed our passion and joined us on our venture. Two years later, with the inspiration from another colaborer in youth ministry, Becky Tirabassi, we put together the first ever conference for women in youth ministry in Chicago. And, now with the faith and help of Liz Duckworth, Victor Books has gone out on a limb to create a resource for women in youth ministry which offers suggestions on the challenges and joys of youth ministry and other related topics.

Being a woman in youth ministry is actually nothing new. In America alone, over sixty years ago, a woman named Evelyn McClusky started the Miracle Book Club in Portland, Oregon, teaching high school students about the love of God. That ministry spawned other ministries by noted individuals such as Francis and Edith Schaeffer, Jim Rayburn, the founder of Young Life, Al Metsker and Jack Hamilton, the founders of the Youth for Christ Club program, and the High School Crusader Clubs of which Bill Gothard later became the director.

Six years later in St. Paul, Minnesota, Marie Marquette founded the Good News Fellowship, a monthly Bible study and encouragement newsletter for young women, with only 20 members. Within one year, she was sending over 3,000 letters a month to young women all over the world. Over the next decade the evangelistic newsletters brought hundreds of young women to the saving knowledge of Christ.

Both these ministries, one local and one international, set the pace for others to follow. And follow they did. Women have been actively involved with Sunday Schools, Pioneer Girls, Awana clubs, church and para-church ministries, and in overseas missions. In fact, it is our hope that volunteer positions continue to grow and evolve into as many shapes and forms as the people that offer them. However, as to women in youth ministry as a professional career, we have to ask why the field has been reluctant to accept women. Perhaps the most basic answer lies in two simple words: *tradition* and *theology*.

TRADITION

Mark Senter explains the youth ministry tradition this way:

> Youth ministry has been predominantly a masculine profession. This is ironic because the originator of the para-church club concept was a woman, Evelyn McClusky. Yet from the time people started being employed to minister to youth, the names on the payroll have been male by an overwhelming majority.
>
> Over the years para-church ministries have become more open to including women on their professional staffs, yet men still dominate all leadership positions and most field staff leadership appointments. Churches from an evangelical tradition are even more closed to women in youth ministry. Few will hire women no matter how qualified unless she is teamed with, and accountable to, a male youth minister. Even the writers and editors of youth publications are male to a greater extent than is found in any other genre of Christian literature. Only in mainline denominations has the door been opened to women in youth ministry.[1]

Men have traditionally been the breadwinners, and women traditionally have held down the home front. However, we do not live in the world of "Happy Days" anymore. Women are interested in, and often may need to, work outside the home. They are seeking meaningful careers. Why not take a love and a passion and turn it into a career? Youth ministry is something that will not only provide personal career satisfaction but it also yields eternal results! Over the last few years we have come to the undeniable conclusion that our students are changing, causing effective youth ministers to adapt as well. "Diversity of leadership" is becoming a key phrase that demands a response. In his book, *The Coming Revolution in Youth Ministry* (Victor Books), Mark Senter concludes: "There is no way in which the tactics currently being used will stem the tidal wave of spiritual, moral, and psychosocial problems faced by the current and coming generations of adolescents" (p. 16). Effective youth ministry can no longer be defined as a Burger Bash and a testimony. Personal relationships through small group interaction are becoming one of the primary catalysts for effective evangelism and discipleship. And to facilitate that type of change we need to develop diverse leaders who can respond to the challenge. In other words, youth ministry *has* to change . . . for the better.

We live in an exciting time. More than ever before there are opportunities for women in the field of youth ministry — especially for entrepreneurial women who have a heart for students and are willing to exercise creative means to reach them!

THEOLOGY

At Journey we are frequently asked by women in youth ministry to theologically substantiate the involvement of women in youth ministry. We encourage seekers to "dig in" to the Bible, as well as other noted books that assist in understanding this topic.

Through study, some individuals *will* change their current positions, and that's fine. The one point that we hope to communicate to you, however, is that as individuals in Christ **we personally are ultimately responsible to Christ** for our theology and values, not to the church elders or para-church board. We encourage you, if you haven't already done so, to do the hard work of challenging your tradition and theology.

Then you need to ask yourself: Am I in the place where I need to be to minister in the way that God has called me to minister? For some, this might mean taking a hard look at where you are and determining what changes need to take place in your life. For others, this exercise might simply confirm your beliefs and your current ministry focus.

As an organization, Journey does not subscribe to any one specific theological persuasion. In fact, we have worked very hard at *not* taking a position. Rather, it is our desire to **help women to be the best youth ministers they can be within their denominational persuasion.**

That's what this book is all about. We hope it will challenge you to think in terms that you perhaps have not considered before. If you are a professional or volunteer woman in youth ministry, you will find a wealth of information uncovering the obstacles and opportunities that are in store for you on this exciting adventure. If you are a man in youth ministry, don't quit reading yet! We have tried to incorporate ideas for effective team ministry, utilizing the partnership concept for improving ministry productivity. In addition, we hope that you will increase your awareness and sensitivity concerning the myriad of challenges that women face, in hopes that you too will become a more effective leader or partner in ministry.

The bottom line is that we hope you will find out more about who you are, how you minister, and ways to be more effective as a team, as you seek to influence students for Christ. **It's all part of the journey!**

Diane Elliot and Ginny Olson

ONE

Beyond Kitchens and Kool-Aid
A theological look at women in youth ministry

by Helen Musick and Karen Thomas

B illy's mother dreaded telling her four-year-old son that Pastor Smith was leaving their small, rural church. Even at a young age, Billy had grown fond of his pastor, who had served the church since before Billy's birth. Denominational leadership had decided to move the pastor to a new congregation miles from Billy's town.

Gently lifting Billy onto her lap, she said, "Billy, I have something to tell you. I know that Pastor Smith has been very special to you. I know you love to walk to the front of the church and listen to the children's sermon each Sunday." She paused, "But Pastor Smith is moving to a new church. This is her last Sunday."

Billy's eyes lost their sparkle. Holding back tears, he replied, "Why, Mommy? I love Pastor Smith. She is so nice. She always gives me a hug after the story."

Billy's mom tried hard to articulate the denomination's decision so that this precious little boy could understand. "Billy, Pastor Smith must help another group of children learn about Jesus." Trying to restore some of his joy, she continued, "But Billy, you are going to have a new pastor. His name is Pastor Bob. He is a very nice man."

Billy's face switched from sadness to bewilderment. He cried, "You mean our new pastor is a *man*?"

"Yes, dear," replied his mother.

"But Mommy," Billy replied with a sense of certainty, "Men can't be pastors!"

In a ministry culture where the leaders are predominately

male, this true story evokes a chuckle. Most people today approach gender roles for ministers much differently than Billy did. Confusion abounds. "A woman pastor? Women can't be pastors!"

As Jesus ascended into heaven, He declared, "All authority in heaven and on earth has been given to me. Therefore go and make disciples of all nations, baptizing them in the name of the Father and of the Son and of the Holy Spirit" (Matt. 28:18-19). The Great Commission has been proclaimed from pulpits and street corners for centuries.

Ironically, a woman who seeks to obey Christ and His commission may find herself in direct opposition to many church denominations' rules of order. Historically, a woman can "make disciples" of children and other women, but not men. And what a heresy if she would even think of baptizing someone! Should we assume that the Great Commission was only a command for men? Must the church differentiate between decrees given to men and decrees given to women? How can church bureaucracy deny women the opportunity to minister when Paul specifically states that in Christ, "There is neither Jew nor Greek, slave nor free, male nor female, for you are all one in Christ Jesus"? (Gal. 3:28)

The debate concerning women in ministry has raged since the birth of the church. In fact, many leading historical theologians' and philosophers' views of women were downright degrading. Aristotle believed that a woman was a "mutilated male" who lacked the substance of soul.[1] Thomas Aquinas noted that women's individual natures were "defective and misbegotten."[2] Immanuel Kant said, "She does not possess certain high insights, she is timid, and not fit for serious employments."[3] The Roman Catholic position prior to the Reformation asserted, "Women are unclean pawns of the devil who lure men to sins of lust." Utilizing Scripture, Martin Luther and John Calvin argued that "both men and women were created in the image of God and therefore stood before God as equals." However, neither Reformer supported women in actual church ministry. Centuries later, the Puritans, Quakers, and Methodists did begin to allow women to preach and teach.[4] Overall, however, women have been banished to the nursery, Sunday School classrooms, or the foreign mission field. Ruth Tucker states, "The debate over women in ministry is really a debate over women and authority. No one argues that women should not have ministry. They may not, however, perform ministry that entails authority — so argue the traditionalists."[5]

When studying the Scripture in its entirety, we can't help but notice God's high value of women, and their equality with males. Jesus' affirming actions toward women were revolutionary in His culture. When Scripture speaks of spiritual gifts, unity and oneness in Christ are emphasized. Gifts are never designated specifically to males or females. Yet, in the work of the church, women are often oppressed and marginalized in such areas as preaching, teaching, administration, prophecy, and apostleship.

As Scripture is the ultimate truth and at the heart of this debate, the focus of this chapter is on biblical texts. We must remember that the Word of God holds authority over human opinion. From the outset, it must be noted that biblical scholars tend to agree that the passages on women in the church challenge their scholarly exegesis. Godly men and women stand on opposing sides of this argument.

CREATION AND CURSE

The creation account of humanity is the starting point of any discussion concerning gender roles. We must remember that both man and woman were created equal "in the image of God." He thought it was "very good" (Gen. 1). This scriptural teaching directly opposed the surrounding culture in which kings were the only ones believed to possess "images of God."[6]

Many fundamentalists point back to the creation to establish the precedent for relational order. James Hurley notes, "Christian worship involves re-establishing the *creational* pattern with men faithfully teaching God's truth and women receptively listening."[7] However, there is no basis for this position in Genesis. Sexual hierarchy did not exist. Man and woman lived in perfect harmony and democracy. Adam stated, "This is now bone of my bones and flesh of my flesh" (Gen. 2:23). Wherever "bone of my bones" appears in the Hebrew Bible it means kinship or similarity, never subordination. The ancient Greeks believed that women were made of inferior material compared to men. Scripture, however, states that women and men were made of the same flesh. Others argue that the male is the superior sex because Adam was created before Eve. This concept is not substantiated, as the order of creation does not grant advantage. After all, the animals were created before man.[8]

Unfortunately, church fathers often took the position that women only possessed the image of God in relation to their husbands. St. Augustine taught, "When she is assigned as a helpmate, a function of that pertains to her alone, then she is not the image of God; but as far as the man is concerned, he is by himself the image of God."[9] In the English language, one may think of a "helper" as a subordinate servant, yet the Hebrew word for helper, *ezer,* refers to strength (Tucker, p. 38). Noted twenty-one times in the Old Testament, *ezer* is used mostly in relation to God as mighty helper. The term never implies subordination.

Women have often been the "scapegoats" for the fall of humanity. Concerning women, Tertullian wrote, "You are the devil's gateway; you are the unsealer of that tree; you are the first deserter of the divine law; you are she who persuaded him whom the devil was not valiant enough to attack. You destroyed so easily God's image, man."[10] Interestingly, in Genesis 2:16-17 God addresses Adam in the plural form of "you," noting that He is possibly speaking to both Adam and Eve. Also, there is no mention of Adam's protest to Eve's action. He also readily eats the fruit.[11]

The fact remains today that all creation suffers the effects of the fall, regardless of blame being placed. The curse upon the female gender is that "your desire shall be for your husband, and he shall rule over you" (Gen. 3:16, NASB). Because Eve overstepped her bounds, now women are naturally plagued with the problem of social dominance."[12] Phyllis Tribble asserts that this curse *describes* role relationships, it does not *prescribe* male dominance.[13] The tense of "he shall rule" is future tense and is used as a prediction or prophecy, not a command.

Jesus ended the curse by taking it upon Himself for humanity. He was born into a world where women were believed to be inferior, yet He allowed them to travel with Him. He praised Mary for sitting at His feet as a theological student. He abolished double standards in adultery and divorce. Instead of blaming women for male lust, He blamed men themselves. In a society where women could not even testify in a court of law, Jesus chose them to be the first to witness His resurrection.[14]

Women and men were created equal, as partners, and helpers. The fall cursed and skewed their relationship, as demonstrated by the extremely patriarchal culture of the old covenant. The reign of Christ, however, reverses the curse and allows equality to reign once again.

WOMEN IN THE BIBLE

Noted biblical egalitarian Faith Martin states, "In the patriarchy, the power of the male over females was direct, personal, and absolute. In each stage of her life, a woman was under the civil authority of a specific man — first her father, then her husband, and, if she was widowed, her son. . . . All males were permanent family members; they had rights, privileges, and future power within the family. . . . Women passed from one family to another, never owning property."[15] From the Old Testament, we learn that women were often used and abused, especially in polygamy. Ceremonial laws were more stringent for females, especially concerning uncleanness and a female's menstruation cycle. Martin asserts that women may not have been priests simply because there were so many days each month, even more if they were pregnant, that they could not appear before the Lord.[16]

Despite the obstacles against women, God powerfully used many women in the salvation history of Israel. Two Old Testament books are named after women. Ruth was the great-grandmother of King David, and Esther saved the nation of Israel. At least five women prophetesses are mentioned in the Old Testament: Miriam, Deborah, Huldah, Noadiah, and the unnamed mother of Isaiah. Deborah was not only a prophetess, she was also a judge and a military leader. Gilbert Bilezikian makes an interesting point when he says, "Abraham is shown as obeying Sarah as often as Sarah obeyed Abraham."[17]

Throughout the New Testament, women were at Jesus' side as they ministered to Him and to others. Phoebe and Priscilla performed administrative and ministerial duties with Paul. In Romans 16, Phoebe is a *diakonos,* which is translated "servant." Interestingly, whenever the same word is used with a man's name, it is translated "deacon" or "minister."

Other noted women in Christian leadership in the first century church include Lydia, Chloe, Euodia and Syntyche, Mary, Tryphaena, Tryphosa, Persis, Eunice, Nympha, and Appia. Philip's four daughters were prophetesses. Eight women are listed in Paul's concluding words in Romans 16. Paul sanctioned women to be deacons (Rom. 16:1), helpers (Rom. 16:2), fellow workers (Rom. 16:3; Phil. 4:2ff), prophets (1 Cor. 11:5), teachers (Titus 2:3), apostles (Rom. 16:7), and possibly also elders (1 Tim. 5:2).

Christian apologist Dorothy Sayers' comments concerning Jesus are worth noting:

> Perhaps it is no wonder that the women were first at the cradle and last at the cross. They had never known a man like this man—there never has been such another. A prophet and teacher who never nagged at them, never flattered or coaxed or patronized; who never made arch jokes about them, never treated them either as "The women, God help us!" or "The ladies, God bless them!"; who rebuked without garrulousness and praised without condescension; who never mapped out their sphere for them, never urged them to be feminine or jeered at them for being female; who had no ax to grind and no uneasy male dignity to defend; who took them as He found them and was completely unself-conscious.[18]

PAUL'S PROBLEMATIC PASSAGES

There are passages in the New Testament that raise questions: "Women should remain silent in the churches," and "I do not permit a woman to teach or have authority over a man." These two statements of Paul's writing, as well as others, are often used to stop women from exercising all of their spiritual gifts. If silence and banning women from teaching are the true intent of these Scriptures, then we immediately bow in obedience to the Word of God. However, in all quality biblical hermeneutics, the context must rule the interpretation. Should women still wear head coverings? Am I in sin wearing jewelry? These particular passages have been interpreted in light of context and culture. Paul's passages must also be examined in their contextual fullness.

Dr. M. Robert Mulholland presents new insights into the Pauline dilemma. He purports that two different paradigms are aligned in Paul's epistles, specifically women relating to men, and wives relating to husbands. He states: The failure to discern these two very different and distinct frames of reference in discussing the roles and relationships of men and women is a major contributor to the apparent discrepancy of the Biblical witness and to the often polarized debate over the role of women in the church."

> Paul's linguistic use delineates the two different paradigms. He always uses the term *gyne* for women and wives; yet he uses *anthropos* for men and *aner* for husbands. Of the fifty-seven uses of *aner* in the New Testament, all except four are used solely for husband with fifteen uses in the problematic passages. Mulholland's thesis will be used as a backdrop to examine each of the passages.[19]

1 Corinthians 14:34-35:

"Women should remain silent in the churches. They are not allowed to speak, but must be in submission, as the Law says. If they want to inquire about something, they should ask their own husbands at home, for it is disgraceful for a woman to speak in church."

First, one must realize that Paul is addressing *wives* in this passage, urging them to address questions to their husbands in private. In the broader context, this was the third group that Paul silenced. In 14:28, Paul silenced those speaking in tongues if no interpreter was available. In 14:29, Paul silenced the prophets so that others could gain revelation. Then, Paul silenced the wives. The problem rested in women capitalizing on their new equality in Christ to initiate issues which should be discussed within the marital relationship. Furthermore, the statement, "it is disgraceful for a woman to speak in church," focuses on marital troubles, as Paul, in 11:5, already fully sanctioned women in public prayer and prophesy.[20]

Furthermore, the church at Corinth experienced chaos in worship. Paul addressed this dilemma, desiring that all would share in exercising their spiritual gifts in an orderly manner. Composed of converted pagans, the Corinthian church needed to continually distinguish itself from the surrounding pagan cults. The pagan women's cults were marked by wild, out of control behavior. Some scholars believe these verses silenced "specific uncontrolled babbling (sacred cries — "lalao") of newly converted Gentile women." Most scholars believe that this was a "limited prohibition." Jews and Gentiles separated the males and females in worship, yet the Christian church introduced worship together. It is probable that some took this freedom beyond its intended limits.[21]

1 Timothy 2:12-15:

"I do not permit a woman to teach or to have authority over a man; she must be silent. For Adam was formed first, then Eve. And Adam was not the one deceived; it was the woman who was deceived and became a sinner. But women will be saved through childbearing — if they continue in faith, love and holiness with propriety."

Linguistically, one must note that the tense of the verb *to permit* is present, indicating a temporary prohibition, not one that is binding for all time. The normal Greek word for authority is *exousia*. However, the word *authentein* is translated "have authority," in this passage and is only used once in the New Testament. Thus, scholars utilized extrabiblical sources to determine the meaning of "to usurp authority" or "to domineer over." Keyes states, "All of the possible meanings indicated negative, abusive and illegitimate actions or attitudes."[22] The message is not that women should have no authority over men, but that they should not abuse, domineer, or usurp authority.

One may feel offended if commanded to learn in silence today because our society values interaction. Yet in Paul's era, sitting in silence under a rabbi was normal. Almost unbelievable to Paul's culture was the desire for women to learn![23] Aida Spencer states, "Silence was . . . a positive attribute for rabbinic students. Paul's words were declaring to his Jewish friends that at this time, women were to be learning in the same manner as did rabbinic students."[24]

The pastoral epistles focus on the theme of heresy and false teaching. One third of 1 Timothy addresses the heresies which were filling the church. Women in the church were propagating Gnosticism, which condemned matter and elevated the spirit and knowledge. They believed that they were receiving special messages from God. Current biblical scholars Richard and Catherine Kroeger state, "Ephesus, incidentally, has been called the bastion of the female spiritual principle in ancient religion. Remember that the group claimed for their prophetesses a special revelation, superior to that afforded to men, and even to Christ." The women speaking out of order were unorthodox heretics who sought to usurp authority with their special revelation. Paul does not prohibit orthodox female teachers, as he notes Priscilla's influence on Apollos and Eunice and Lois' influence on Timothy.[25]

Creating myths and genealogies was a favorite Gnostic pastime, with the creation story as their specialty. Often, they would reorder creation to place woman first in the creation order and impart wisdom to Adam. Understandably, one sees why Paul must recount the creation narrative in 1 Timothy. Furthermore, Gnostics also believed that women should strive to become like men, denying marriage and childbearing. In so doing, good spirits would no longer have to reside in evil flesh. Paul was refuting this teaching and elevating femininity in 1 Timothy 2:15. Women, like men, are saved by grace through faith in Christ Jesus alone.[26]

Another problem passage is found in 1 Timothy 3 where Paul lists the qualifications of an overseer. First, one must note "If one holds this literally, it also rules out all single men, like Paul and Jesus. Polygamy was a common practice among Jewish and Gentile men. Women did not participate. Thus, the exhortation, "the husband of but one wife," was necessary.[27]

1 Corinthians 11:3-12:
"Now I want you to realize that the head of every man is Christ, and the head of the woman is man, and the head of Christ is God. . . . And every woman who prays or prophesies with her head uncovered dishonors her head . . . the woman is the glory of man. For man did not come from woman, but woman came from man. . . . In the Lord, however, woman is not indepen-

dent of man, nor is man independent of woman. For as woman came from man, so also man is born of woman. But everything comes from God."

Scholars admit that this is one of the most difficult passages to interpret in the entire corpus of Scripture. In the Greek, man is *aner,* signifying that the passage focuses on husbands and wives, not men and women in a church setting. Furthermore, a "veil" in the Roman-Hellenistic world was worn by married women to signify their unavailability.[28] The word for head in Greek is *kephale,* which does not mean authority, but "source or origin" Contextually, this agrees as the passage concludes with "everything comes from God."[29] Traditionalists view the "head" concept as one of rulership and domination. The body submits to the thoughts and actions of the head.

However, Fred Layman contests this concept. He states, "To begin with, the function of the head (brain) in rational processes was not known prior to the rise of modern science. The ancients didn't have the remotest idea of the function of the brain and the nervous system and attributed psychical functions to the soul, the spirit, or to other parts of the body—the heart, the bowels, the kidneys, the bones, etc.—but never the head."[30] The headship of Christ to the church is seen as self-sacrificing, cherishing, and nurturing. The relationship of mutual submission between husband and wife was revolutionary to the culture. In Christ, the curse of male domination and female subordination was broken. Freedom was restored for all.

WOMEN LEADERS IN CHURCH HISTORY

Beyond Scripture, there have been many women in leadership positions within the church. Noted Christian historian Philip Schaff writes, "It should not be forgotten that many virgins of the early church devoted their whole energies to the care for the sick and the poor, or exhibited as martyrs a degree of passive virtue and moral heroism altogether unknown before."[31] Vibia Perpetua was one of the most well-known early female martyrs in North Africa. The monastic life provided opportunities for many women to exercise their faith and charity. The Reformation ushered in a new biblical view of women, yet did nothing to alter their status within the church.

Women found freedom in almost every sectarian movement following the Reformation. Women were given equal status in the Quaker church from its inception. John and Charles Wesley's mother, Susanna, was noted as a "preacher of righteousness." Catherine Booth cofounded the Salvation Army alongside her husband. Clarissa Danforth preached at revivals throughout New England in the nineteenth century. Jerena Lee, a black revival minister with the African Episcopal Church, led many to saving faith. Evangelist Maggie Van Cott was often compared to Dwight L. Moody, bringing thousands to faith each year. The most well-known female evangelist of the nineteenth century was Phoebe Palmer, "Mother of the Holiness Movement." She traveled internationally, with an estimated 25,000 conversions.

The mission field opened wide to women as church denominations realized the need was greater than the "man" power available. Tucker states, "Few of these mission leaders even contemplated the inconsistency of denying women ministry in their own homeland while encouraging such ministry abroad." Unfortunately, some missions which were once open to women are now closed.[32]

THE CALL AND COMMISSION

To go back to our opening story, Billy thinks that only women can be pastors. Is that fair to men? Many think only men can be pastors. Is that fair to women? We know that Scripture supports the equal distribution of gifts and the call to obedience in using them. The command to "Go and make disciples" is a universal call for both males and females. The prophetic words of Joel, which Peter declared fulfilled on the day of Pentecost, remind us of this. "In the last days, God says, I will pour out My Spirit on *all* people. Your *sons and daughters* will prophesy, your young men will see visions, your old men will dream dreams. Even on My servants, *both men and women,* I will pour out My spirit in those days, and *they* will prophesy" (Acts 2:17, 18, emphasis added).

Both of us [Helen and Karen] grew up in Protestant homes with religious parents who were committed to teaching us the ways of Christ. However, neither one of us was exposed to women in full-time ministry until we reached our twenties. We both wonder how our lives would have been different if we had had a female youth pastor or mentor earlier in our lives.

The body of Christ is crying out for women leaders who desire to minister faithfully with the talents God has given them. Youth today need positive role models of both genders for healthy relational development and deep understanding of the call of Christ. Speaking of the servant who did nothing with the talents given, Jesus declared, "You wicked, lazy servant!" (Matt. 25:26)

May each of us faithfully and unashamedly walk out the call and commission placed on our life, praying fervently that we will one day hear Jesus say, "Well done, good and faithful servant!"

BARRIER BREAKERS

1. **How have you been exposed to women in Christian leadership?**

2. **How do you wish your exposure had been different?**

3. **What are the passages in the Bible that are difficult for you in light of the topic of women in ministry?**

4. **What, or who, has been most influential in developing your biblical stance of women in ministry?**

Authors

Name: *Karen Thomas* (right)

Occupation: *Student in final year studies for the Master of Divinity degree from Asbury Theological Seminary*
Birthplace: *Decatur, Indiana*
Current home: *Wilmore, Kentucky*
Marital status: *Married*
My favorite food is: *Grilled chicken caesar salad*
The last movie that significantly impacted me was: It's a Wonderful Life
A good book that I would recommend is: The Henrietta Mears Story — *especially for women in ministry*
I've never been able to: *Do a cartwheel or flip*
I'd give anything to meet: *Billy Graham and Mother Theresa*
If I could change one thing about myself: *I would like vegetables more than sweets*
I'm working on: *Living a balanced life*
If I weren't in youth ministry, I'd be: *Working in public relations or management for Walt Disney World*
Words that best describe me are: *Enthusiastic, leader, sensitive, spiritual*
The thing that I love about youth ministry is: *The twinkle in the eyes of a student when they catch a glimpse of a new truth*
One of my passions is to: *See others grow in their love for Jesus*
I've learned that: *Surrender is the key to living a Christlike life and truly the basis for ministry. It's a daily journey and it does not come easily, but it's always right and a blessing once the step is taken.*

Name: *Helen Musick* (left)

Occupation: *Mom, wife, youth ministry volunteer, speaker, teacher, writer*
Birthplace: *Pensacola, FL*
Current home: *Louisville, Kentucky*
Marital status: *Married*
Children: *Nathan (5), Laura (4), Will (1)*
My favorite food is: *Italian*
The last movie that significantly impacted me was: Philadelphia
The style that best reflects me is: *Traditional with a contemporary flair*
A good book that I would recommend is: The Mystery of Christ and Why We Don't Get It!
If I could do it over: *I'd never kiss any man except the one I married!*
I'm working on: *Being more patient and praying more for my children*
If I weren't in youth ministry, I'd be: *An airline stewardess*
Words that best describe me are: *Encouraging, friendly*
I love to: *Go on a vacation and be pampered*
It really bugs me when: *I have to wait in line*
The thing that I love about youth ministry is: *The impact I have on someone's future*
My favorite place to spend time with God is: *At the table in the kitchen early in the morning*
One of my passions is to: *See abortion laws reversed*
If there is one thing that I would like to tell my colleagues it would be: *Put your best energy into the relationships closest to you.*
I would like to be remembered for: *Caring about people the way Jesus cared for people*

TWO

Maximizing Our Differences
How a woman ministers differently than a man

by Kara Eckmann

T ypical woman speaker."
        Statements such as these always intrigue me.
        "What do you mean?" I asked my friend sitting next to
me. We had just heard a woman speak to over 400 teenagers
about the importance of prayer.

"Well," he continued, "her voice was whiny and she wasn't
very funny."

I vehemently disagreed with my friend's broad generaliza-
tions, but I had heard them before. All of my life I have stood
against gender stereotypes. I have constantly corrected peers
and teenagers who begin sentences with phrases like "Men
always . . ." or "Women never. . . ." Yet those types of comments I have heard so often left me wondering, *are there differences in the way men and women communicate? If so, what
are they?*

After observing hundreds of men and women communicate in large group, small group, and one-on-one settings, I have
concluded that there are differences. These are not absolute,
nor inevitable. Rather, they are tendencies. Trends. At this
point, scientific research has not proven conclusively whether
these variances are due to biological and physiological factors or
cultural and sociological ones. Nonetheless, I believe differences do exist.

To the women reading this book, do you know that men do
not talk to each other in bathrooms? Or that high school guys
dread sharing a bed with another guy at summer camp? To the
men reading this book, do you know that teenage girls visit the

bathrooms in packs? Or that high school girls pack for summer camp in total confidence that they will borrow clothes from other girls in their cabin?

Of course, these are only superficial differences. But there are differences that pierce deeper. These are the ones that color the way we communicate and the way we minister. If we don't understand and maximize them, we will always be handicapped. However, if we do understand them and use them to our advantage, we will be one step further in leading both young men and women toward the ultimate goal, Jesus Christ.

THE WOMAN IN FRONT OF THE CROWD

Think for a moment about the last youth ministry conference or leadership seminar brochure that you reviewed. I hope women were included in the speaker lineup. But, chances are, most (if not all) of the keynote speakers were men.

Now think about the guest speakers and preachers who have taught in your church or youth ministry. Most were probably men.

Finally, think back to the last summer camp you attended. In all likelihood the general session speaker, as well as most of the seminar speakers, were men.

When we women observe the scarcity of female speakers, we can use this challenge to our advantage or to our disadvantage. We can become angry and respond by verbally attacking and criticizing others. We can become frustrated and complain about how unfair and how difficult it is to be a woman in leadership.

Our other option is to use this scarcity as an advantage. Although there are difficulties in being a female communicator, we have the advantage of being in greater demand, because there are fewer of us. There are tremendous resources available for us to learn how to be more effective communicators. Because there are less expectations and stereotypes of female speakers, we have the freedom to be creative in our teaching and preaching.

Finally, as Christian women, we have an advantage when

we realize that our ultimate source of speaking and leadership authority is not in ourselves, but in Christ alone. As believers we are merely a tunnel through which the Holy Spirit moves to change the hearts and minds of the audience.

If you feel called to speak, teach, or preach, be encouraged! The Lord is strengthening and empowering this generation of girls and women to assume unprecedented speaking roles. Although it varies across denominations and geographical regions, He is raising up female voices to proclaim His truth and serve as living, visible examples for others.

Recently, I was apprehensive about speaking at a large youth gathering. I called a friend in youth ministry to ask for prayer. She was very understanding and encouraged me. "Kara, just think, there may be girls sitting in the audience who have never heard a female speaker. Your example will show them that women can speak and lead."

I hung up the phone less anxious and more in awe of God and His desire to speak to His people through His women.

MAXIMIZING THE DIFFERENCES IN WHAT WOMEN SAY

Please remember that this chapter is not designed to perpetuate stereotypes, but to propel women forward as communicators. I'm convinced that God wants to use today's women to share His word with teenagers. This will happen as women, as well as men, use their own personalities and gifts to their advantage.

Captivate the Audience

At this time in history, hundreds, if not thousands, of voices are clamoring for teenagers' attention. In the first thirty seconds of any talk, you need to prove that your voice deserves their attention. Just because you plan to say something doesn't mean your audience plans to listen.

All speakers must create a reason for their audience to *want* to listen. This is especially true of female speakers. A typical audience consists of basically three types of people: those who support female speakers, those who are neutral about female speakers, and those who oppose female speakers. A speaker quickly needs to earn the trust, or at least the respect, of those who fall into the last two types. According to Ruth Herrman Siress in *Working Woman's Communications Survival Guide,* the introduction is important in earning respect because it builds rapport with the audience. It also establishes the speaker's style and tone, subject matter, and credibility.[1] The introduction gives the audience its first glimpse of who the speaker really is.

There are four typical formats for an introduction. The first and most frequently used introduction in youth settings is humor, which we'll explore in the next section. A second (also frequently used) format is relevancy. In this approach, a speaker quotes from recent movies or song lyrics, or discusses a recent news event or shocking statistics. Third, speakers can use a dramatic introduction by sharing an interesting and moving story about themselves or others. Finally, speakers can directly involve their audience by breaking them into smaller groups or asking questions to get their opinion.

Most of these formats share one characteristic: each raises a need. Once when I was struggling in developing an introduction, I came across Ephesians 4:29 in my morning devotions. "Do not let any unwholesome talk come out of your mouths, but only what is helpful for *building others up according to their needs,* that it may benefit those who listen" (emphasis added). A strong introduction will bring the audience to a point of thinking, "This meets a need in my life. I will *choose* to listen."

In addition to raising a need, a strong introduction is well-planned. The opening sentence and paragraph need to be thought through ahead of time. A good idea is to begin with enthusiasm. Avoid beginning with a stream of "thank yous" such as, "Today I'd like to thank Laura for inviting me here and Matt for the ride here and Jim for. . . ." It's never a good idea to begin with apologies and phrases such as, "I'm sorry. I'm not as ready as I'd like to be . . ." or "I have to apologize for not really knowing what I'm going to say. . . ."

A carefully crafted introduction shows the audience that this talk is important, to the speaker and to the listeners.

Include Humor

There is probably no better way to *gain* a youth audience's attention than through humor. There is also probably no better way to *keep* a youth audience's attention than through humor.

Yet, it seems that many female speakers steer away from using humor. Many women find it awkward and uncomfortable. Perhaps it is because men are accustomed to being the clowns and the center of attention, or perhaps it is because women have unconsciously decided that humor is more masculine than feminine. Regardless of the cause, the end result is the same: female speakers seem to use less humor in public speaking.

Folklorist Carol Mitchell did a systematic study of joke telling among college students. She found that college men told most of their jokes to other men, but they also often told many jokes to mixed groups and to women. In contrast, women told most of their jokes to other women and very few jokes to groups that included men. Also, men were more likely to tell jokes in a group of four or more people, while women were more likely to tell jokes in a group of three or less. In groups of four or more, women often flatly refused to tell a joke and instead promised to share a joke later in private. Unlike men, women hesitated in telling jokes in front of people they didn't know well. Men never refused the invitation to tell jokes.[2]

According to Ken Davis, the President of Dynamic Communications International and a recognized communicator and humorist, "One reason including humor may be more difficult for women is because of what is required in traditional slapstick humor. The exaggerated body movements and facial expressions are often considered unwomanly."[3]

Humor is too important in building a bridge between the speaker and the audience to neglect altogether. The trick for a female communicator is to develop her own sense of humor. Everyone has one. The key is to find it and fine-tune it. Maybe you are a strong joke teller. Maybe you can tell stories about outrageous, uncommon events or stories about typical, everyday life. Or maybe your humor is more sophisticated and intelligent. Davis has observed many marvelous female humorists who "make me laugh out loud. Whether it's their timing or a surprise twist in a story or a witty remark, women can and are using humor to communicate."[4]

Ask your close friends to help you identify and develop your own unique sense of humor. Practice telling stories or jokes in small groups before you stand in front of a crowd. Forced humor is awkward, but natural humor will always win with an audience.

Feel Free to Feel

An effective speaker is a passionate speaker. An effective speaker shows her or his own feelings about the topic.

Showing feelings in front of groups tends to be easier for female speakers than male speakers. Often a male speaker will describe how he's feeling by making statements such as, "This angers me" or "I am thrilled about this idea." But a female speaker is more likely to actually show her feelings. She will laugh, she will sigh, she will smile, or she will cry.

If this describes you, you have an advantage. Not only will you be able to explain how you're feeling, but you'll also be able to display how you're feeling. In most cases, your emotion will engage the emotion of the audience. Your pain becomes their pain. Your fear becomes their fear. Your zest becomes their zest. Your grief becomes their grief.

A word of caution is in order here: too much emotion may be distracting. For example, a speaker with too much enthusiasm can seem fake or shallow. Too many tears can move an audience to disgust, not empathy. Make sure that the emotion is appropriate and genuine. If you pause for a moment before your expression of emotions, you will prepare your audience, and they will be more likely to be gripped by your feelings.

Be Clear

An outstanding talk combines emotions and feelings with clarity and facts. Unfortunately, over the last fifty years, women speakers have been noted primarily for their ability to share from their hearts, not for their ability to share from their minds. They have been commended for the way they teach from their own life experiences, not for their strong biblical theology.

In an interview with *Journey,* Lynn Ziegenfuss, the National Training Director of Youth for Christ commented, "Many women speakers restrict their message to their testimony.

I believe that a testimony is a wonderful way to communicate truth about God's faithfulness. But I also believe that a woman can offer substance beyond her testimony."[5]

Ken Davis agrees,

> Unfortunately, many women have fallen into the stereotype of what I call the "Church Lady Syndrome." The "Church Lady" lives. I have seen her. She uses phrases such as, "Isn't it precious" and communicates more from emotion than content. She may have the right motivations, but she is avoiding the hard work of communication.[6]

Female speakers need to expand their speaking beyond their testimonies. Use Scripture as a foundation and personal experiences as illustrations, not the other way around. When teaching from Scripture, be clear. I've heard it said that, "A mist in the pulpit becomes a fog in the pew." The comprehension of the audience is often in direct proportion to the clarity of the speaker.

Davis provides hints on how to organize a talk. "Clarity is a matter of preparation. Every speaker must know where he or she is headed. This means not only answering the question, 'What do I want to talk about?' but '*Why* do I want to talk about it?' In other words, you need to know exactly what you are trying to accomplish with your talk."[7]

In addition to a clear sense of purpose, a good talk will also have a clear point of application. Every talk should answer the "So what?" question. When speaking to teenagers, don't assume that they can develop their own personal application. Include applications for them. The more the better.

Finally, a good talk will have a clear conclusion. Many conclusions resemble an airplane circling a runway, just looking for a place to land. Select a powerful and memorable way to end the talk. Have only one conclusion, not several. Make a lasting final impression. Then sit down!

MAXIMIZING THE DIFFERENCES IN HOW WOMEN SAY IT

Up to this point we have focused solely on actual words. However, effective speakers know that the audience is convinced not only by what they say, but also by how they say it. Although female speakers have to work a little harder at commanding the attention of the audience, there are practical steps that will pay off. These principles apply to any speaker, whether male or female.

Positioning

Make sure that where you stand stands out.

You may remember an incident involving President George Bush and Queen Elizabeth of England in the early 1990s. It was a dignified and stately ceremony in which both the President and the Queen were scheduled to deliver a speech from the same podium. First, President Bush delivered his eloquent speech as he stood tall and dignified behind the podium. Queen Elizabeth followed him and stood at the same spot behind the same podium. Because the Queen is about twelve inches shorter than the President, all the audience and television cameras could see was the Queen's hat! While the President commanded attention, the Queen seemed miniscule and rather comical.

Shorter women can learn a valuable lesson from Queen Elizabeth and beware of tall podiums! Even taller women can learn to move away from the podium and closer to the audience. It's best to have nothing as a barrier between you and the audience. This gives the audience the feeling that the speaker is confident and in control.

Make sure that the audience can see you. An audience will quickly lose interest if they cannot see your face. Your face should be well lit. In addition, the background or wall behind you should draw, not distract, people's attention to you. Make your audience's wandering eyes want to focus in your direction.

Voice

Even more frustrating than not being able to see a speaker is not being able to hear her. As a general rule, female voices have a higher pitch than male voices. This makes it more difficult for women to project over a large room or group of people.

You cannot change your voice, but you can magnify it. Perhaps you should consider purchasing a small portable sound system. An investment of a few hundred dollars could transform your ability to attract and keep a crowd's attention.

When speaking to an audience of more than forty people, try to use a sound system if at all possible. It gives more control. It reminds the audience that their attention should be riveted on the speaker.

Posture
One of my friends was just beginning to speak regularly in front of large groups of people. Before each talk, she prepared and prayed diligently. However, she is of medium height and tends to slump over when she speaks. Instead of approaching the audience in confidence, she gave the impression of withdrawing in fear.

One of her coworkers encouraged her to stand up straight and step as close to the audience as she could. That simple step has transformed her effectiveness.

When speaking, stand up straight. This does not mean being absolutely, perfectly vertical, but it does mean that you should stand erect with confidence. Of course, you can occasionally lean toward the audience to draw them into what you are saying. But general posture should be standing straight with an air of confidence.

Gestures
In every preaching class I took in seminary, I noticed that the women tended to gesture less than the men. When women did gesture, their gestures were small, close to their body, and fairly limp.

Women, take note: gesture and gesture boldly. If you are explaining something exciting, throw your hands up in the air. When you introduce your first point, hold up one finger. When you want to draw more attention to what you are saying, punctuate it with swift hand motions.

When you gesture, move your hands away from your body. Make your hand motions brisk and precise. If you're unsure when or how to gesture, observe other speakers and decide what is appropriate for you. Then practice gesturing in front of a mirror until it feels comfortable. It may never feel completely natural, but your animation will accent the message you are communicating.

Attitude

Every speaker projects an attitude. A speaker may seem nervous, hostile, unsure, or tired. His or her attitude shines through. I've observed that most female speakers fall into one of two categories: either too timid or too cocky.

The most effective attitude that a female speaker needs to communicate is confidence, mixed with humility. The *confidence* comes when you view yourself as God's messenger for this group at this particular time. You have prepared and prayed and are fully ready for the speaking challenge that lies ahead.

Confidence also comes from practice. Think about enrolling in a college speech class or attending the local "Toastmasters" speech club to fine-tune your skills.[8] Ken Davis agrees, "If you want to learn to communicate, look for every opportunity that will help you demonstrate and develop your skills." After all, practice may not make perfect, but it will lead to greater self-assuredness.

The *humility* comes when you realize the responsibility that you carry when you speak. The Lord has entrusted you with the privilege of leading and influencing the group that sits before you. Deep inside, you realize that the only lasting effect of your words comes from His anointing and blessing.

The humbling reality is that in six months most of the students will have forgotten the exact words you spoke. However, what they will remember is the overall impression you conveyed to them and the impact of the Holy Spirit speaking to them through you.

THE WOMAN IN A SMALL GROUP

Most female youth workers spend more time interacting in small groups than they do speaking before large groups. Even though I speak in large group settings once or twice a week, I interact with others in small group settings and meetings at least twice that often.

At the adult level, I am often the only woman. Whether it's with our church's pastoral staff, or youth workers in my community, or our youth ministry worship band, I am often the only female. As the only woman, I don't feel inferior. I simply feel different. But I have learned several key ingredients that help create a productive and healthy group dynamic.

Speak Up with Certainty

I've noticed something rather alarming about myself. I hesitate to speak up and share my ideas in a small group setting dominated by men.

I first noticed this three years ago in a planning meeting for a Southern California conference. I had new ideas about how the conference could be organized, but when surrounded by four men, I kept my ideas to myself. Ironically, the men in the group eventually discovered those identical ideas for themselves and adopted and implemented them successfully.

Although I have become more vocal in small group settings with men in the past few years, I still catch myself hesitating. A few weeks ago in a board meeting for a citywide conference, I was once again the only woman surrounded by men. It was a new setting and I only knew about half of the men present. I had input to share that would help shape the direction of the conference, but I didn't feel comfortable sharing it. I think the coordinator realized my predicament because he asked me, "Kara, what do you think about this idea?" At that point, I felt comfortable sharing my opinions. But it was only after he asked me that I spoke freely.

I am not alone. Scientific research confirms three interesting differences between men and women in small group settings, two of which emerge from the same study by psychologist H.M. Leet-Pelligrini. Her first finding was that women interrupt and contribute less than men, even when they have greater expertise and experience. Leet-Pelligrini videotaped small groups and pairs as they discussed the effects of television violence on children. Some of these groups were all women, some all men, and some mixed. In certain cases, she actually made one of the members an expert by providing relevant factual information and time to read and assimilate it before the discussion.

Leet-Pelligrini expected that the member with the greatest expertise would talk more and interrupt more. This turned out to be true, except in the cases where the woman was the expert and the man was the non-expert. In these situations, the woman took less leadership in the conversation, preferring instead to offer phrases such as "Yeah" and "That's right" in response to the opinions of the non-expert male. As a result, observers often labeled the male non-expert as more dominant than the female expert.

In addition to contributing and interrupting less, Leet-Pelligrini's second finding was that the women also had less control over conversations. When an expert man talked with an uninformed man, he dominated the conversation in the beginning, but not always in the end. The man who lacked information would question and challenge the expert man and possibly gain control of the conversation. But when an expert man talked to an uninformed woman, he took a controlling role in the beginning of the conversation and kept that role until the end. The woman seemed to accept the reactive role once she realized that the man she was talking to had more information on the subject.[9]

Scientific studies indicate a third significant difference between men and women in small groups: the conversation's topic and style tend to gravitate toward men's preferences. In a study conducted by Alice Deakins, she observed people's conversations during lunch hour in a dining room. The men and women in Deakin's study were all bank officers, functioning as equals at work. Deakins observed that male gatherings tended to focus on business, the food they were eating, and sports, while female gatherings tended to focus on relationships, business, and weight control.

When the men and women ate together, they tended to avoid the topics that each group liked best and instead discussed topics of interest to both. But, in discussing these topics, they adapted the style of the men alone. The group would discuss recreation the way the men did, focusing on sports and vacations rather than exercise or health, as the women would when they were alone. Similarly, they talked about housing in the way the men did, focusing on location, property values, and commuting time instead of the interiors of houses and finding cleaning help, as the women did when they were alone.[10]

The same trends can be demonstrated in adolescents. After analyzing tape recordings of private conversations among teenagers, Deborah Lange observed differences in conversation topics between same-sex groupings. When girls were alone, they talked primarily about problems in their interpersonal relationships; when boys were alone, they talked about activities and plans, and made comments about friends. When boys and girls talked together, they talked about activities and plans, and made comments about friends. Basically, when boys and girls talked together, they talked in the same manner and style as the boys did when there were no girls present. In other words, the girls adapted their conversation topics and style to the boys. [11]

The fact is that women do not need to fit into the mold of the men in your small groups and meetings. In *You Just Don't Understand: Women and Men in Conversation,* Dr. Deborah Tannen challenges,

> Women who find themselves unwillingly cast as the listener should practice propelling themselves out of that position rather than waiting patiently for the lecture to end. Perhaps they need to give up the belief that they must wait for the floor to be handed to them. If they have something to say on a subject, they might push themselves to volunteer it. If they are bored with a subject, they can exercise some influence on the conversation and change the topic to something they would rather discuss. [12]

Women should also be encouraged with one advantage they have in small group interactions: women tend to value unity and a sense of teamwork more than men. In a study by Marjorie Harness Goodwin, she found that young boys became leaders when they gave orders and got others to follow them. In contrast, young girls demonstrated a preference for egalitarian leadership. They began proposals with words such as *Let's* and *We* to gather consensus and agreement from the entire group. In addition, when a girl did make a leadership decision herself, she was much more likely than her boy counterpart to explain to the group why she made such a decision. [13]

This emphasis on teamwork may make it easier for women to create an atmosphere that is cooperative instead of competitive. Women can help create a synergistic environment in which the contribution of the group members working together is greater than the sum total of its individual parts. One word for this is *alignment,* the process by which each group member commits to an agreed goal. Instead of group members jockeying for powerful positions, they can learn to serve and listen to one another.

Sit Comfortably and Professionally

The same principle holds true for small groups as large groups: it's not just what you say, it's how you say it.

Perhaps you've observed the differences between male and female sitting posture. Men tend to sprawl out, make themselves comfortable, and take up as much space as possible. In contrast, women tend to draw themselves in and take up as little space as possible.

This difference is noticeable between men and women in airplane or movie theater seats. If there is an armrest between a man and a woman, the male will almost always assume control, even if the woman sitting next to him is a total stranger!

In observing male sitting posture, Elizabeth Aries found that men sprawled out in the same way, regardless of whether there were women present. When women were by themselves, they seemed to feel comfortable to sprawl out as the men did. However, Aries noticed that when women were in the same room as men, they drew themselves in, assuming "ladylike" postures.[14]

THE WOMAN ONE-ON-ONE

Whether it's with another youth worker at a conference or a student at a nearby fast-food restaurant, much of youth ministry happens one-on-one. But are these times being maximized to their potential? Read on to learn how to reap the most possible fruit from one-on-one times.

Balance between "Rapport Talk" and "Report Talk"

I've noticed a difference between the offices of female and male youth workers. Women often intentionally set up "sitting corners" with two chairs facing each other. This is so they can interact with others in a less intimidating, more welcoming environment. Their priority is building rapport with the other person.

Men rarely arrange their offices like this. They prefer to interact with someone across a desk. They maintain control and authority. It's less intimate. It's safer.

According to Dr. Tannen, this difference is due to the different preferences of men and women in one-on-one conversation. As a rule, men prefer "report talk" in which the two parties focus on facts. The goal is to identify the problem as well as the best solution as quickly as possible.

In contrast, women prefer "rapport talk." They talk about problems to discuss them, not necessarily to solve them. They don't desire resolution as much as they hunger for a listening ear.[15]

When I discuss my personal needs and problems with my closest male friends, I notice that often their quick response is to ask the question, "What can I do to help?" or "What can you do about it?" When I discuss these same problems with my female friends, their response is more often something like, "I know how you must feel and I'm sorry."

As a youth worker, regardless of our gender, we need a healthy balance of both report talk and rapport talk. All ministry boils down to relationships, so rapport talk is essential. Yet our responsibility is also to intervene in the lives of teenagers with practical advice.

Ask yourself, *right now, what do I do more of in one-on-one settings — report talk or rapport talk?* Now ask yourself, *what do I need to do more of?* Remember your answers to these two questions the next time you meet with someone one-on-one and adjust your approach accordingly. Also, when meeting with a student, evaluate what her needs are and adjust your conversation as needed.

Beware of Two Dangers

In one-on-one settings, women need to beware of two dangers. Danger number one: the tendency to avoid conflict.

Many women fear face-to-face confrontation. Even Oprah Winfrey, a well-known television talk show host who confronts people every day on her show, admits,

My biggest flaw is my inability to confront people. After all the shows I've done, the books I've read, the psychologists I've talked to, I still allow myself to get ripped off to the *n*th degree. It takes me days and days of procrastinating and agonizing before I can work up the nerve to say anything."[16]

The reverse is also true. It's not only women who don't want to confront people; people don't want to confront women. In the last month, two male students, at separate times, have told me that they don't want to confront an adult female leader because they "don't want to make her cry."

Avoiding conflict is avoiding part of leadership responsibility. Jesus teaches in Matthew 18:15, "If your brother sins against you, go and show him his fault, just between the two of you." Similarly, in Ephesians 4:15, Paul admonishes that we are to speak "the truth in love." In the same way, we are to listen openly to others when they approach us with their opinion or their perspective on a situation, even when it differs from ours. A true leader is a true listener. A true listener is someone who listens when what she hears is difficult and combative, not only soothing and complimentary.

The second danger falls on the opposite end of the relational spectrum from conflict. It's the danger of a male student or coworker having an unhealthy romantic crush on a female in leadership. After all, a female youth worker may offer a male student or adult the type of friendship and fun that they have never had before.

To fight against this danger, we need to set healthy emotional boundaries. As women we need to watch how much of our personal lives we share with male students one-on-one. We also need to trust our intuition about whether a student or volunteer is becoming too attached.

Part of setting healthy emotional boundaries is setting healthy logistical boundaries. This may mean not having one-on-one meetings with male students in isolated areas. Instead, choose to meet in public areas such as restaurants or shopping malls. If an office does not have windows, think about leaving the door partly ajar. Yes, a degree of the privacy is lost but there is an assurance of seeking to avoid the appearance of evil.

Another commonsense rule is: don't give a male student a

ride home by yourself. Recently, I told a seventeen-year-old male that I could not give him a ride home. This meant that one of our male staff had to drive thirty minutes out of his way, instead of me driving about thirty seconds out of my way. Even after I explained my position to both the male student and the male staff member, part of me felt foolish for asking this staff worker to drive so far out of his way. But my gut feeling was that I had made the right choice. I don't believe that anything would have happened, but it's better to make wise decisions and have no regrets. After all, many students come from confused and dysfunctional backgrounds. I'm not advising paranoia, but I am advising caution.

We also need to take the same precautions with female students. Unless you know a girl and her family well, it's also best never to be in isolated areas with her alone. In this age of accusations and lawsuits, women need to protect themselves from anything that might appear to be inappropriate.

CONCLUSION: A NEW ERA

Regardless of the size of the setting, women are emerging as communicators and leaders. Old patterns and stereotypes are being shattered. Women are pioneering new paths in youth ministry communication.

I often think of a recent graduation speech by former First Lady, Barbara Bush. While giving the commencement address at Wellesley College, an all-women's college, Mrs. Bush proclaimed, "Who knows? Somewhere out in this audience may even be someone who will follow in my footsteps and preside over the White House as the President's spouse. And I wish him well."

The Wellesley crowd rejoiced. And so can we, as new doors in youth ministry are being opened for women, and women are walking through them.

BARRIER BREAKERS

1. What differences have you noticed between male and female communicators?

2. How can you gain more practice and experience in speaking before a crowd?

3. Do you find yourself hesitating before sharing your input and ideas in small groups? If so, how can you overcome this tendency?

4. The author states, "As a youth worker, regardless of our gender, we need a healthy balance of both report talk and rapport talk." What is your style? Do you need to work on being more balanced?

Author

Name: *Kara Eckmann*

Occupation: *Director of College Ministries at Lake Avenue Congregational Church in Pasadena, California*
Birthday: *August 6, 1970*
Birthplace: *Japan*
Current home: *San Diego, California*
Marital status: *Single*
My favorite food is: *Fish tacos*
The last movie that significantly impacted me was: What's Eating Gilbert Grape?
The style that best reflects me is: *"Express"*
I've never been able to: *Whistle*
If I were a famous painter I'd paint: *Beach scenes*
If I could change one thing about myself: *I'd rest more*
I'm working on: *Surviving the Ph.D. program at Fuller Seminary*
If I weren't in youth ministry, I'd be: *An attorney with political aspirations*
Words that best describe me are: *Laughter, fun*
I love to: *Go to movies*
I really don't care for: *Chocolate*
The thing that I love about youth ministry is: *Seeing God transform lives*
One of my passions is to: *See women develop their leadership gifts*
People always think I'm: *Busy*
If there is one thing that I would like to tell my colleagues it would be: *Relax and enjoy students*
I would like to be remembered for: *Knowing Jesus and making Jesus known*

THREE

Ministry Would Be Great If It Weren't for the People

Effective team ministry

by Laurie Polich

> *Two are better than one, because they have a good reward for their toil. For if they fall down, one will lift up the other; but woe to the one who is alone and falls and does not have another to help.* (Ecc. 4:9-10, NRSV)

I believe in team ministry.

Having said that, I am the first to admit that team ministry is difficult. Sometimes we find ourselves quoting the biblical concepts of spiritual gifts (in 1 Cor. 12) while struggling like crazy to hang in there with our fellow workers. We recognize our need to function as a body, but sometimes we wish the mouth wasn't so loud nor the hands so tightly grasped. Clashing personalities and power struggles don't help matters when we are already facing the pressures of ministry itself. And yet it is in the team context that Christ has called us to do His work. Together.

In my ministry work, I've certainly had my share of struggles with team ministry, but I've also experienced wonderful benefits. Believe it or not, the times that I have grown the most often occurred when I had to work with people who were very different from me. God used these people to sharpen me and make me more effective.

Team ministry is an introvert working with an extrovert, a visionary working with an administrator. An encourager working with a prophet. All kinds of people. People that make a community, working in harmony with other communities, thus functioning as the larger body of Christ.

CHRISTIAN COMMUNITY

God not only wants to work through us, He wants to work in us, and He uses community to shape us into the people He wants us to be. We can reject this process because it involves pain and difficulty. But if we do, we are the ones who lose. If we can persevere, even through difficult times, we will begin to understand what it really means to be a part of the body of Christ.

In *Life Together,* Dietrich Bonhoeffer reminds us:

> The serious Christian, set down for the first time in a Christian community, is likely to bring with him a very definite idea of what Christian life together should be and to try to realize it. But God's grace speedily shatters such dreams. Just as surely as God desires to lead us to a knowledge of genuine Christian fellowship, so surely must we be overwhelmed by a great disillusionment with others, with Christians in general, and, if we are fortunate, with ourselves.[1]

Notice that Bonhoeffer says it is God's *grace* that shatters our dreams. When we allow our dreams to be shattered, then God can replace them with His dreams, which are always far superior to ours.

Bonhoeffer goes on to say,

> Only that fellowship which faces such disillusionment, with all its unhappy and ugly aspects, begins to be what it should be in God's sight, begins to grasp in faith the promise that is given to it. The sooner this shock of disillusionment comes to an individual and to a community the better for both. A community which cannot bear and cannot survive such a crisis, which insists upon keeping its illusion when it should be shattered, permanently loses in that moment the promise of Christian community.[2]

When we become a part of a community, one of the first things we notice is our differences. These differences are well described in *The Delicate Art of Dancing with Porcupines* by Bob Phillips. While this is a secular book, we can apply these personality types to the individuals functioning within the body of Christ as well. Phillips suggests that there are four basic personality styles: the Driver, the Analytical, the Amiable, and the Expressive. Perhaps the best way to describe them is to give two examples from the book that show how the styles function at work and at play.

Imagine that each of the four social styles purchased a swing set, which requires assembly, for his children. The Analytical takes all the parts out of the box and lays them in neat order. Next he reads the directions very carefully and assembles the swing set precisely by the numbers. The Driver dumps all the parts in a pile on the ground, then begins assembling the swing intuitively. If he encounters a problem, he may look at the directions, but only as a last resort. The Amiable reads the instructions and then hires someone else to put the swing together for him. And the Expressive does not read the instructions at all. Rather, he goes next door to his Analytical neighbor and talks him into putting the swing together for him.

At a social gathering like a party, the Analytical will usually spend his time with only one or two people. The Driver will move into a group and slowly overpower it. If the Amiable moves into a group, he will usually take part by actively listening. Sometimes Amiables will not even join groups, choosing instead to sit on the sidelines and watch people. They like to study human behavior. The Expressive will enter a party mouth first and will most likely talk to everyone at the party before he leaves (pp. 54–55).

From these illustrations you can get a rough idea of your own personality style, as well as those of the people on your ministry team. Because youth ministry involves working together on programs and events, as well as building relationships with students, these examples serve us well in describing how different personalities function in our ministries.

Our personalities dictate the ways we approach a person or a task. Some of us place higher priority on the person, thereby neglecting the task (Amiable and Expressive). Others of us place a higher priority on the task, sometimes to the neglect of the person (Analytical and Drivers). Some are more comfortable working with small groups and individual relationships (Amiable and Analytical). Others thrive while leading large groups and running events (Expressive and Drivers).

The fact is that we need all four personality types to construct an effective ministry team. In 1 Corinthians 12:14-23 Paul gives us a wonderful illustration:

Now the body is not made up of one part but of many. If the foot should say, "Because I am not an eye, I do not belong to the body," it would not for that reason cease to be part of the body. . . . If the whole body were an eye, where would the sense of hearing be? If the whole body were an ear, where would the sense of smell be? But in fact God has arranged the parts in the body, every one of them, just as He wanted them to be. If they were all one part, where would the body be? As it is, there are many parts, but one body. The eye cannot say to the hand, "I don't need you!" And the head cannot say to the feet, "I don't need you!" On the contrary, those parts of the body that seem to be weaker are indispensable, and the parts that we think are less honorable we treat with special honor.

DIVERSITY WITHOUT DIVISION

Paul's vivid illustration in 1 Corinthians 12 of the different parts of the body shows us how our community suffers when we reject one another. The challenge, then, is to learn to embrace our uniqueness. Diversity will create tension and conflict. That's inevitable. However, when a conflict arises, we have two choices: we can reject each other and break the team apart or, recognizing our need for one another and the strength we give to one another through our diversity, we can strive to work together.

I remember when I started at First Presbyterian Berkeley. I inherited a number of volunteers who had worked with the previous youth pastor. I was pleased when they chose not to leave their ministries, thus providing a consistency for the students.

However, it didn't take long for them to realize that I'm very different from the youth pastor who preceded me. One of the fundamental differences was that I am a woman. In addition, my strongest gifts were teaching, leading discussions, and relating with kids. I was not as detail oriented as my predecessor. We'd plan a trip, tons of kids would sign up, and I would find myself saying, "Oh yeah, I guess we need some way to get there." My forte was not keeping track of permission slips, getting the right number of tents, and making sure all the drivers had a map.

I learned quickly that, although by nature I'm not detail orientated, some details are too important to miss. As the leader, I needed to develop other team members to keep track of the details for me. I learned to let others walk alongside me and let their strengths become ministry assets.

It's humbling to recognize our weaknesses. I think it is natural for us to want to be good at everything. We fear criticism so we try to do everything right.

Soon we find we are spending less time doing the things we are genuinely good at, and more time doing the things that are hardest for us to do. Over time, we either burn out and leave ministry altogether, or we learn an important principle about ministry: we are not meant to minister alone. What sets ministry apart from other jobs is that the workers are put together to function *supernaturally* as a body.

Paul puts it this way:

> Just as each of us has one body with many members, and these members do not all have the same function, so in Christ we who are many form one body, and each member belongs to all the others. We have different gifts, according to the grace given us (Rom. 12:4-6).

Notice the verse does not say, "Each of us have all the gifts, according to the grace given us." It says, "We all have different gifts." We are called to work together. We are one in Christ, but our oneness is shaped by our differences. It is through these differences that we are changed more and more into the image of Christ.

Galatians 3:28 indicates that these differences are secondary to our unity in Christ. Nevertheless, we have to face the fact that these differences do exist.

I can still remember the first real conflict I had with one of my youth advisers. We were at a Christmas party for the senior highers, and I could tell she was upset with me. We went into the next room to talk. When I asked her what was wrong, she exploded. Her frustration centered on my lack of organization and my inability to see important details. She concluded by basically saying, "It's amazing anything ever happens in this ministry." Needless to say, it wasn't one of my high points as a youth director!

After mentally dealing with my own anger and defensiveness, we were able to finish our conversation by agreeing that it was quite possible she was brought to this ministry for the very reason she was ready to leave it. She was able to see my weaknesses because they were her strengths. God had brought us together because we needed each other to do His work. Our differences, not our similarities, brought us together. Our challenge was to realize that our gifts would not only be used to minister to kids, but to sharpen one another.

Often we miss out on this important aspect of Christian community because we find that overcoming our differences is a difficult process. We imagine community to be supportive and nurturing, but the reality is that it can also be challenging and sharpening.

One of the best times I ever had with my staff was when we divided up into groups by our personality styles and told the other styles what we wish they understood about us. It was a time of laughter, healing, and growth. We learned not to look at our differences with judgment, but to look at them as God's grace to make us better than we ever could be alone. That is what team ministry is all about!

BARRIER BREAKERS

1. Describe the uniqueness of the individuals on your ministry team.

2. What do you bring to the team?

3. What are the most common challenges that arise in your team?

4. What are ways that your team supports each other?

Author

Name: *Laurie Polich*

Occupation: *Youth director at First Presbyterian Berkeley, Associate Staff of Youth Specialties*
Current home: *Albany (Berkeley), California*
Marital status: *Single*
My favorite food is: *Peanut butter, frozen yogurt, and poppyseed muffins*
The last movie that significantly impacted me was: Schindler's List
The style that best reflects me is: *Unconventional*
A good book that I would recommend is: A Testament of Devotion *by Thomas Kelly*
Nobody knows I'm: *Half Serbian*
If I were a famous painter, I'd paint: *People*
If I could change one thing about myself, I would change: *My hair (you asked)*
I'm working on: *A proposal for a book*
If I weren't in youth ministry, I'd be: *An actress*
Words that best describe me: *Sensitive, fun loving*
I love to: *Eat, exercise, and create (not necessarily in that order)*
If I could go anywhere in the world, it would be: *Around the world (that's my dream!)*
The thing that I love about youth ministry is: *Kids — honestly*
One thing that I could live without ever doing again is: *Bungee jumping*
My favorite place to spend time with God is: *In the mountains or by the water*
One of my passions is to: *Listen to jazz*
I've learned that: *Pain is part of the deal*
If there is one thing that I would like to tell my colleagues, it would be: *Be yourself and let God use you*

FOUR

Dynamic Duos
Partnerships that work

by Mike DeVito and Kara Eckmann

Youth ministry thinking has turned a corner.

In past decades, a frequent focus of discussion has been if women could, and should, work alongside men in key leadership positions. Now the focus of discussion is changing from *if* to *how*. In other words, the key question is becoming, "How can men and women in youth ministry best work together to make an impact in the lives of students?"

If you've been in a close ministry working relationship, you know it can be challenging — regardless of gender. In this chapter, we want to focus on the enormous advantages of working with someone of the opposite gender and how teamwork can affect the lives of your students.

After all, we shouldn't let ourselves be robbed of the opportunity to work together. Men and women work together effectively every day in other careers. Youth ministry is a great place for God to creatively use the best assets of both genders.

OUR STORY

Mike:
Perhaps one reason we feel so strongly about male/female partnership is because of our own story. My call to youth ministry began my senior year in high school and was confirmed during a summer church internship following my college graduation in 1975. Four years later, while serving as a youth pastor at a church in Oregon, I was intrigued by the high quality of leader-

ship and speaking by women in paid youth ministry positions at a nearby church. It was at this point that my conviction that women needed to be in influential and visible youth ministry positions began to grow. As I had seen women in action, I believed that God desired to elevate women who would surpass the traditional and stereotypical leadership roles of taking the minutes and passing out snacks at meetings.

Kara:

I was a junior in high school in Mike's youth ministry. I had just lost an all-school election for student body president and needed somewhere to focus my abilities and gifts. Mike, recognizing my leadership potential, asked me to serve on his student leadership team. I quickly got involved. Before I left for college, Mike met with me in his office and challenged me, "Someday you're going to catch a vision for youth ministry. Just be ready."

Up to that point, I was planning to study to become an attorney. I had encountered only a few professional women in youth ministry until I went with Mike and other students to a youth seminar. During a break at that seminar, I was approached by a woman who was part of the seminar's leadership team. Three sentences into our conversation, the woman asked, "Have you ever thought about going into youth ministry?"

I answered, "Sort of. I'm debating between that and becoming an attorney."

The woman replied, "I don't usually ask people if they're going into youth ministry. But, I think this is a divine appointment. Here's my card. Please call me. My name is Becky Tirabassi."

The encouragement from Becky was part of the development of my vision for youth ministry. During my undergraduate studies at Stanford University, I served as a senior leader for a Young Life group near the college campus. I met several other Christian leaders who echoed the need for more women in ministry. During my summers, I returned to my home church to assist Mike as a summer youth intern. In my private times of prayer, my burden for reaching teenagers was growing. By my senior year in college, I was certain that God was calling me to youth ministry.

Mike:
While Kara was away at Stanford, I started planting seeds in the minds of the other pastors of my need for a female partner in ministry. Three months before Kara's graduation, the seeds took root and the church board decided to invite Kara to work alongside me as the youth ministry assistant. Kara accepted. We were both thrilled.

That was three years ago. It has been exciting to see dreams come true from the early days of Kara on the student leadership team, to now working side by side.[1] More than ever, we are both convinced that God wants to raise up dynamic duos of men and women who are committed to love and serve students together.

Although there is no magic recipe for creating a dynamic duo, we have found three ingredients to be absolutely essential. All three are rooted in Scripture and all three have practical implications for the birth and growth of a ministry partnership: serve, support, and complement.

"ME LAST"

The first ingredient in creating a dynamic duo can be described by the phrase, "Me Last." In an era that idolizes and promotes self-centeredness, authentic ministry partnerships must be grounded in selflessness. As leaders, we are called to imitate Jesus' example of giving up our rights and saying, "Me Last" not "Me First." As the Apostle Paul explained to the Philippians, "Your attitude should be the same as that of Christ Jesus: Who, being in very nature God, did not consider equality with God something to be grasped, but made Himself nothing, taking the very nature of a servant" (Phil. 2:5-7).

Note the last word: *servant.* Certainly Paul didn't mean to limit this scriptural mandate to be a servant to the Philippians. Servanthood is an attitude that permeates New Testament teachings and examples of leadership. It is an attitude we should continue to model today. Jesus Himself proclaimed that He "did not come to be served, but to serve, and to give his life as a ransom for many" (Matt. 20:28).

True ministry partnership is founded on a servanthood that expresses itself through an attitude of both the mind and the heart. Servanthood of the mind means that we intellectually recognize our duty to support our partner. It means knowing that we should serve. In contrast, servanthood of the heart means we experience joy and are energized when we come alongside and support our partner. It is wanting to serve. Authentic partnership comes alive when the mind and heart intersect, and we experience the true joy of laying down our life for others.

Day to day interactions and ministry tasks provide ample opportunities to live out the "Me Last" philosophy. In working with a partner, there needs to be an awareness of his or her needs, whether big or small. Big needs can be assuming responsibility for a youth service or event because your partner needs a night off. It can be stepping in to help finish last minute details for the upcoming retreat. A small need may be passing out pencils, turning out lights, or making photocopies. Regardless of the size of the task, the important thing is that each partner is aware of the other's needs and is determined to do what is required to meet those needs.

A great chance to practice the attitude of "Me Last" is on the road. Together, we took a group of students to DC '94, the Youth for Christ super-conference on evangelism, held in Washington D.C. During one night of sightseeing, Kara became very ill. Feeling some responsibility for the group, she continued on until they stopped for dinner at a fast-food restaurant. Realizing how sick she was, Mike looked at her and said, "Kara, you don't have to be here. I think you should go back to the hotel and get some rest." Grateful, Kara complied. This was Mike's chance to serve.

In addition to meeting a partner's needs, much of the servanthood experienced in a dynamic duo comes through sharing. Partners need to begin by sharing the authority and ownership of the ministry with each other. In our case, Mike was the youth pastor, Kara was the assistant. Mike was clearly the person ultimately in charge, but he knew that his long range goal was to give the ministry away. When it came to making decisions, we made them together. If we disagreed, we tried to consider the other person's perspective and strengths. Sometimes this meant Kara supported Mike's opinions. At other times, Mike relinquished his authority as youth pastor to allow Kara to develop her own ministry ideas and programs. This was because Mike was convinced that the ministry was first the Lord's and then it was his to share with others.

As we have learned to share ownership of the youth ministry, we have also learned to share the adventures of working with teenagers. This means sharing not only the good stuff, but the hard stuff too. For us, the good stuff is made up of the special times we share with students — McDonald's, late hours at overnighters, and summer missions trips to name a few. Plus, we share the thrill every June of hearing "Pomp and Circumstance" as we watch our students walk across a stage to receive their high school diplomas, knowing that together, we have made an investment in the life of one more student.

Youth ministry involves more than smiles and cheers, however. It also involves heartache and tears. For us, the hard stuff has come as we have shared in students' crises. Whether it be loneliness, family conflict, pregnancy, or divorce, we have had to learn to walk together as we step in to listen, counsel, and support students and their friends and families.

Our most difficult crisis was the tragic murder three years ago of one of our students, a fifteen-year-old girl. Christin was one of our student leaders and met with Mike's wife in a discipleship group. The trauma of her murder was compounded by the fact that she was the fourth girl from our youth ministry to die in a two-year period. Together we visited the funeral home and helped her family plan her memorial service. Beyond the logistical issues, we shared the difficulty of trying to answer students' hard questions, support our volunteer youth staff in their concern for students and in their grief, and deal with our own grief as well.

Interestingly, both the good and hard stuff have matured our partnership and enabled us to minister more effectively together. We have had to grow by getting involved with people and their problems. We have learned how to balance each other emotionally to ensure that we have enough stamina to persevere. We have become more sensitive to the needs of individual

students and their families and have held each other accountable for our shared goal of valuing people more than programs.
In short, the sharing of the good and hard stuff has helped us
realize the importance of making and sharing memories with
students that will influence them for the rest of their lives.

"YOUR NUMBER ONE FAN"

We all need fans. Hopefully you have some close friends and
family members who can cheer you on in the midst of youth
ministry's challenges. In addition to our wonderfully supportive
family and friends, we have found each other to be our greatest
fans.

Admittedly, at no point in Scripture are we ever exhorted
to "be someone's fan," but we are expected to cheer each other
on. In Hebrews, we are challenged, "And let us consider how
we may spur one another on toward love and good deeds"
(Heb. 10:24). Developing a dynamic duo requires an intentional commitment to support and lift up one another. This is the
second ingredient for a successful dynamic duo.

Just as the day-to-day interactions of ministry are full of opportunities to live out the "Me Last" philosophy, they are also
the perfect time to let your partner know that you are his or her
"number one fan." Here are some ideas:
1. Give your partner that "I'm on your team" look in the
    midst of a chaotic event or meeting.
2. Leave an encouraging message on his answering ma-
    chine before or after a tough event.
3. Ask your partner, "How can I pray for you?" Then really
    pray for her. And let her know you're praying for her.
4. Remind him, "You can do it," when he feels
    overwhelmed.
5. Enlarge the fan club by asking students to write notes of
    encouragement.

Pick one idea and try it. Or make your own list of ways to let
your partner know that you are on his or her team. Be creative.
The success of your partnership depends on it.

Ironically, the success of your partnership depends not

only on being a number one fan but on simultaneously maintaining a healthy sense of separation. If you've been around youth ministry for long, you've heard the horror stories. Male youth workers who satisfy their cravings to feel loved, secure, and significant through inappropriate relationships with female partners. Female youth workers whose commitment to building a strong partnership with their male ministry counterpart evolves into a relationship plagued with fuzzy boundaries and romantic tension. Being in ministry together is a passionate adventure, and it's all too easy for the passion to spill over into inappropriate areas. Whether you are single or married, these are very real issues with very real and potentially disastrous consequences.

Boundaries
If you are committed to developing a dynamic duo, please be likewise committed to the following safeguards. Begin by looking at your working relationship realistically; after all, it is a *working* relationship. Be honest with yourself in acknowledging any unhealthy feelings of attraction you may have toward your partner. Make sure you have someone hold you accountable who is relatively removed from your ministry setting and can offer honest and objective feedback. If you're struggling, sometimes sharing these struggles with your ministry partner can only fan the flame of potential sparks, so share your struggle with him or her sparingly and with caution, if at all.

Other practical steps include avoiding spending excessive amounts of time together, especially late at night. We also recommend praying for your partner's dating or marriage relationships. Finally, become a fan of your partner's family in more visible and direct ways. Although Kara is single, she is committed to maintaining a supportive friendship with Mike's wife and two daughters so that she can be a 100 percent fan of his entire family.

A real danger in developing a close working relationship is that those outside of it can feel excluded. After all, you spend hours during the day discussing ministry problems and situations with your ministry partner; the last thing you want to do when you go home at night is to discuss them all over again with your spouse or roommates. However, they need to feel included, and you need to hear their perspective. As you work to strengthen communication ties with your ministry partner, be as intentional in strengthening your communication in your other significant relationships.

Conflict Resolution

In addition to being committed to a healthy and appropriate relationship, a youth ministry dynamic duo must be willing to work through the inevitable conflicts that arise. Begin by identifying in your own mind the exact cause of the conflict. Make sure you consider both sides of the issue. Then, find the right time to communicate your thoughts to your partner. As a general rule, sooner is better than later, but three minutes before your youth service begins is probably not the ideal time.

Once you've found the right time, give your partner full eye contact. Listen carefully. In explaining your position, always remember that it's better to be kind and right than just right. After all, you are each other's fan. You want each other to succeed, and you want your ministry partnership to succeed as well.

Besides looking for the right time, look for the right place; a place away from others. Your youth staff meeting is neither the time nor the place for you to challenge your partner on the poor planning of last night's pool party. You can talk it out later.

To be honest, our conflicts have been few and far between, but as we reflect on the tensions that have existed, the root problems are poor communication and distorted expectations. Our most recent conflict came during the planning and programming of an annual denominational youth convention. We spent hours brainstorming program ideas, including drama, video, music, computer graphics, and the actual weekend schedule. We discussed the jobs that needed to be done and divided the responsibilities between us. Apparently, we didn't discuss our responsibilities clearly enough because in the middle of the program, there were gaping holes and Kara felt alone in filling them. If Kara had clearly expressed her concerns before and during the event, Mike would have willingly volunteered to help. Instead, Kara's frustration with the event, and with Mike, snowballed. Reflecting together on times such as this reminds us that early and direct communication, as well as clear expectations, are foundational to avoiding and resolving conflict.

Avoid Jealousy

Jealousy can creep into even the most supportive of partnerships. Don't allow it to eat away and undermine your foundation. Don't let Satan steal the joy of celebrating your partner's victories. Bring it out into the open by discussing your feelings with your partner. And remember that you are His and that your ministry is His.

Maybe it's not you who is in conflict with your partner — it's someone else. Imagine that your partner was obviously not ready for the crowdbreaker. Or an entire bus of students has to wait in the cold because your partner misplaced the camp contract. Others are noticing the mistakes. They are coming to you with their complaints and criticism.

It's easy to feel as if you're in the middle. On the one hand, you may want those coming with criticism to feel they've been heard. But on the other hand, you want to support and not undermine your partner. What do you do?

The best answer is to try to have both sides speak with each other directly. Avoid taking sides. Those with criticism should personally go to your partner. Avoid taking sides, however; remember that your relationship with your partner will likely last longer than the criticism will. For this reason, you need to communicate publicly to your partner, and all others involved, your loyalty and commitment to the duo. Later, in private, you can help your partner answer the question, "What can I learn from this criticism?" True fans will not only communicate enough to avoid mistakes but will also communicate honestly enough to learn and grow from mistakes.

"HANDING OFF THE BALL"

The exciting thing about a partnership is that we're not just fans cheering each other on, we're on the same playing field. As you learn to move through issues of jealousy, failure, and conflict, your partnership matures. Trust is earned. You come to value your partner's strengths and gifts and realize when it's the right time to hand the ball off to them. Your partner is then free to excel in his or her own skills and expertise.

In 1 Corinthians 12:18-20, Paul writes, "But in fact God has arranged the parts in the body, every one of them, just as He wanted them to be. If they were all one part, where would the body be? As it is, there are many parts, but one body." From this, we learn that a ministry partnership is made up of two or more people who need each other.

God has made us unique individuals. The adventure comes when we, as partners, help discover what we do well and how our specific gifting complements one another. In addition to serving and supporting one another, when we learn how to complement one another effectively, we multiply our impact in the lives of students.

For example, Mike has strong prophetic and motivational gifts. On the other hand, Kara tends to be more merciful and empathetic. If we feel a student needs to be listened to, Kara intervenes. If we feel a student needs a strong challenge, Mike takes the ball. Understanding these differences only strengthens our ability to minister to students.

The same type of balance has even occurred in writing this book chapter. Mike's strengths in writing are creativity and conviction; Kara's strength in writing is clarity. As we have written these pages, we have laughed as Mike enthusiastically throws out ideas and concepts and Kara tries to add the structure.

The real test of how well we complement each other comes when we shop together. We enter a store with a list of the youth ministry supplies we need. Kara purposefully heads straight for the supplies we have specifically listed, while Mike's creative "shopping juices" begin to flow. He's often interested in everything *but* what is on the prepared list. While Kara is calculating whether it is more cost effective to purchase Hershey's Kisses or M & M's for a retreat snack, Mike is captivated by the newest electronic signs, decorations, notepads, and other potential youth ministry gadgets. It is only after much experience that we have learned to appreciate our differences and realize the balance that we bring to our youth ministry.

The truth of Solomon's teaching, "As iron sharpens iron, so

one man sharpens another" (Prov. 27:17) is definitely alive in our idea exchange. Two heads and hearts have proven to be better than one as we have brainstormed everything from conference programming to the location of a poster to various approaches in a counseling situation. At times if one of us feels tired or loses momentum in an idea discussion, we will actually say to the other, "You take the ball," and then watch as the other person continues a string of "What if we . . . ?" brainstorming ideas.

The challenge for any dynamic duo that enjoys working together can be such a strong dependency that one partner feels inadequate without the other. We saw symptoms of this in our working relationship when we were both involved in both the junior high and senior high leadership at our church. Sure, we loved working side by side, but we came to realize that our time and energy would be spent more effectively if we divided and conquered. Kara stepped into more leadership in junior high and Mike took the ball in senior high. There was still the opportunity to share ideas related to both age levels, but it was better for us, as well as for our students, to split responsibilities. After all, a partnership that recognizes and values each person's strengths and gifts makes for the strongest possible team.

CONCLUSION

When all is said and done, why is a dynamic duo in youth ministry necessary? As we have lived out our ministry adventure together, we have realized that, although it is crucial that we serve, support, and complement each other, that is not the bottom line.

The bottom line is the impact that a dynamic duo can have on the lives of students.

Two students come to mind immediately. They have been in our youth ministry since seventh grade. They both graduated from high school last June. Both now attend the same southern California Christian college. They both want to go into youth ministry. In the midst of all of these similar experiences, there is one major difference between these two students: Aaron is male and Rina is female.

Dynamic duos exist for students such as Aaron and Rina. Not only is God calling Aaron and Rina to serve Him as individuals in youth ministry, but He is also calling them to seek after their own dynamic duo relationships. Our hope is that they have learned that two leaders can strengthen and complement each other. In other words, we hope they have learned what Christ has called all of us to do: work together for the building up of His kingdom.

BARRIER BREAKERS

1. Are you currently in a ministry relationship that you would describe as a dynamic duo? If not, is there anyone who may eventually fill that role?

2. How can you practice the attitude of "me last" by sharing and serving your ministry partner?

3. We've identified poor communication and distorted expectations as the root problems of our conflicts. What would you identify as the root problems of conflict in your team? How can you overcome these conflicts?

4. What in your ministry is difficult for you to hand off to others on your team? What will it take for you to learn to relinquish these responsibilities?

Author

(See Kara Eckmann p. 51)

Name: *Mike DeVito*

Occupation: *Southern California Coordinator of National Network of Youth Ministries*
Current home: *San Diego, California*
Marital status: *Married eighteen years to Kristi*
Children: *Two girls, Candice (15), Kimberly (11)*
The style that best reflects me is: *"The Gap"*
A good book that I would recommend is: Mere Christianity
If I could do it over: *I would be a basketball player*
I'd give anything to meet: *Billy Graham*
If I were a famous painter, I'd paint: *I wouldn't be one. I hate painting — just ask my wife.*
If I could change one thing about myself: *I would have a tougher skin and softer heart*
I'm working on: *What I want to be when I grow up*
If I weren't in youth ministry, I'd be: *A tennis instructor*
Words that best describe me are: *Intense, fun, passionate*
If I could go anywhere in the world, it would be: *Maui*
It really bugs me when: *People can't be trusted*
The thing that I love about youth ministry is: *Discipling students*
One thing that I could live without ever doing again is: *Going to the doctor*
People always think I'm: *Busy*
I've learned that: *You've only got one shot at this, so give it your best*
If there is one thing that I would like to tell my colleagues, it would be: *We've got to work together*
I would like to be remembered for: *Being a servant*

FIVE

Choose Your Own Adventure
Women in various seasons of ministry

by Kara Eckmann with Eilleen Rollerson, Lisa Walker, and Nancy Wilson

Y ou never knew where you would end up.

That was the beauty of the children's book series *Choose Your Own Adventure*. My brother and I would spend hours devouring book after book. From the opening page of each story, we were assigned the identity of the main character, the "hero," whose goal was always the same — defeat the opposing evil forces. At the bottom of each action-packed page, we were faced with two different courses of action. Our choices determined which page we turned to next, which ultimately determined the hero's destiny.

Interestingly, this childhood series in many ways parallels youth ministry. Each of us is a "hero" of sorts, seeking to stand for Jesus and defeat the enemy. At every fork in the road of life, we make choices that take us down different paths. Some of us are walking on the path of singleness. Others of us have chosen the path of marriage. Some have decided to add children to the journey. Many are volunteers; some are paid for our work with youth.

Regardless of life stages, we can be encouraged and equipped by other "heroes" who walk similar paths. They can help point us in the right direction and help us to navigate through challenging terrain.

We interviewed five women across the country who have chosen different ministry adventures. As they share their insights, we hope to learn from their successes, and maybe more importantly, from their struggles. We hope that the Lord will use this chapter to strengthen and encourage each of you on your own adventurous journeys.

ADVENTURE NUMBER ONE
Ministry as a Single Woman: Nancy Wilson

 There is, perhaps, no other woman in youth ministry with nationwide influence who delights in the adventure of singleness more than Nancy Wilson. Nancy's twenty years of ministry experience with Student Venture, the high school outreach ministry of Campus Crusade for Christ, began in Indiana in 1975 as a campus field worker. From there, she became a women's trainer, then a Student Venture traveling representative, and, finally, the National Women's Coordinator. She now lives in Florida and serves as Student Venture's Associate National Director, a position that enables her to focus on Student Venture's women's ministry, international ministry, and prayer.

Question:
Nancy, in your opinion, what are the advantages of ministering as a single woman?

Nancy:
The number one advantage and joy that ministering singlely brings is an undistracted devotion to Jesus Christ. I have complete freedom and flexibility in my schedule to pursue my relationship with the Lord. He is my number one priority and focus.

A second advantage of being a single in ministry is my freedom to respond to opportunities and invitations to travel and minister. I have been very blessed with the opportunity to travel all over the United States and the world sharing the Gospel with young people and encouraging other youth leaders. This is one of my favorite aspects of my job! These trips have expanded my vision for the Lord's work and the strategic role I believe this generation of youth can play in the completion of the Great Commission.

Question:
Tell us about a highlight of your experience as a single youth worker.

Nancy:

Well, in addition to my international travels and speaking opportunities, my other great joy is the fun of working with my associates, both men and women. I grew up with four brothers, and I absolutely love men and enjoy working with men. God has made men and women to complement each other. A complete ministry happens when we're working hand in hand and actually seeing our different strengths unite to produce the most creative and effective ministry possible.

Question:

Do you think your coworkers treat you differently because you are single?

Nancy:

I greatly appreciate my coworkers because they understand and embrace my intensity about my sense of purpose and mission. They have not bought into the false stereotype that as a single woman, I am incomplete and waiting around for marriage. Instead, they reinforce God's calling in my life.

There is the assumption that because I am single, I can do more. I have no restraints, no restrictions. I can travel to the extra city, I can handle the extra responsibility. Though this is partially true, I also believe it is important that I maintain balance in order to prevent myself from burning-out or being all ministry-minded and not cultivating outside interests that will only enhance my long-range ability to minister.

Question:

What are some of the hardest times you have faced as a single youth worker?

Nancy:

To be very honest, one of the hardest times was my recent fortieth birthday. I've always been incredibly optimistic and excited about the future, full of vision and dreams. But when I turned forty, suddenly my future seemed to weigh a little heavier on my shoulders. I looked around at all the younger women coming into the ministry and began to wonder what the future would hold for me. I've had to lift that burden up to the Lord and choose to trust that He knows the future and has a great and perfect plan to maximize all the experiences He has given me. My responsibility is to continue to unwrap and develop the gifts He has given to me and expand and grow in new ways. Focusing on Him and the privilege of helping to fulfill His Great Commission renews my sense of destiny.

Question:
Do you ever feel lonely?

Nancy:
Not as often as you might think. The ministry keeps me quite busy, and my life is filled with wonderful friends and family. However, it can be hard when my close coworkers get married and no longer work with me. Or I can tend to feel lonely after a big event where I've poured my heart and soul into something and had almost constant contact with people. After giving out so much spiritually, physically, and emotionally, I sometimes desire a single, close intimate relationship.

Question:
How have you responded to these feelings of loneliness?

Nancy:
Well, in both unhealthy ways and healthy ways. My most unhealthy response is to become too introspective and try to analyze my lonely feelings. This analysis can become a downward spiral that plummets me further into feelings of anxiety or depression.

To counter this, I have developed a policy called "glance and gaze." I glance at my problems or my emotions, but then I fix my gaze back on Christ.

Another healthy response to my loneliness is what I call "reaching up and out." First of all, I reach up to the Lord, inviting Him into my loneliness and drawing close to Him for He promises in James 4:8, "Draw near to God and He will draw near to you" (NASB). He has never let me down yet. Reaching out means initiating fun activities and building relationships with other people. For me, being outdoors and enjoying sports is particularly refreshing and rewarding.

Question:
Have you felt disappointed, or let down by God, because you are not married?

Nancy:
Actually, I can't say that I have ever felt disappointed or let down. By His grace, I've been able to receive my singleness as a "gift" from the Lord. Though there have been times when I have wondered if I am missing out on something, overall I'm confident He has designed a unique and special plan for me. One of my favorite passages is Psalm 118:8-9, "It is better to take refuge in the LORD than to trust in man. It is better to take refuge in the LORD than to trust in princes." The Lord has given me a treasure to have Him alone to turn to as my partner.

Question:
Are you saying that you look to the Lord as your husband?

Nancy:
Absolutely. He is my partner. When I think about a husband-wife relationship, I think of oneness. I am thrilled with the oneness in purpose, in emotions, and in dreams that I share with the Lord as my husband. As I grow in oneness with the Lord, what is on His heart will be on my heart. What He is concerned about, I will become concerned about. I become a partner in His purposes.

Question:
Nancy, what tips would you give to other single female youth workers?

Nancy:
First and foremost, cultivate intimate relationships with the Lord and with others. God has promised to meet all of your needs, including your need for relational intimacy. If He has not given you a husband, then He desires to meet this need Himself and through open, vulnerable friendships with other women.

Second, guard your heart and your affections. Recognize when and how you are emotionally vulnerable. Know yourself and prepare yourself so that you can respond correctly when you're feeling lonely or dealing with physical desires. Have godly women hold you accountable and stand with you in prayer during your temptations.

And then, use discretion with your male ministry partners. Set healthy boundaries. For me, this means that I don't travel with my married male coworkers nor do I counsel with them in private. If I need to meet with a married man, I will do so with my office door partially open or at a crowded restaurant. It is crucial that we avoid the appearance of evil. God honors this discretion, and uses it as an example to the girls and younger youth workers who are watching.

Finally, enjoy life! What a privilege to have the time and energy to devote to ministry. Take advantage of the opportunities that God brings. Develop your gifts and abilities and take risks. Try new things. Grow with the Lord and with others. Life is just too short and eternity is too long to waste time worrying about where Prince Charming is. After all, Jesus is the perfect Prince.

ADVENTURE NUMBER TWO
Ministry as Partners with Your Husband: Lisa Walker

Your telephone rings. The parent calling asks to speak to the youth director. You and your husband look at each other, wondering which one of you should take the call. After all, you are codirectors of your church's youth ministry.

For Lisa Walker, this situation is not hypothetical; it is her day-to-day reality. She and her husband, Steve, have been full-time codirectors of the youth ministry at Saint Margaret Mary Catholic Church in Winter Park, Florida for the last five years. They are responsible for both junior high and senior high and spend much of their time on the Confirmation process for their ninth graders as well as the annual national Orlando Heart Catholic Workcamp.

Question:

Lisa, you and your husband's job descriptions indicate that you should have a full and equal partnership. Is this really true?

Lisa:

Totally. Steve and I have a true partnership. We share all aspects of the ministry. We believe that the Lord has called us together to be full partners in ministry.

Question:

If you had to pick just one highlight of your ministry together as a couple, what would it be?

Lisa:

There are so many, but if I had to pick one it would be a letter we received this year from a student who was in our youth group years ago. She had quit coming to the youth group in her junior year, and in her own words, she was traveling down "some bumpy roads." Her parents' divorce as well as her own immoral choices were causing her much pain and confusion. She has come back to the Lord, and she thanked Steve and I for together pointing her back to Him. In her words, during her parents' divorce, we were her "spiritual parents." This was real affirmation for our call as a couple in ministry.

Question:

Can you imagine being in youth ministry and not working side by side with Steve?

Lisa:

Well, we tried before and it was chaotic. Having two youth groups, two volunteer teams, and two separate summer trips left very little time for us to be together. Now that we have two children, I can't even imagine what it would be like to have two separate youth ministries.

Question:

What difficulties do you and your husband face as a couple in full-time ministry?

Lisa:

We live and breathe youth ministry. It can become the center of most of our conversations. It gets to be a little much when we are in bed discussing the youth group meeting!

To counter this, we schedule "dates" together and make a conscious effort to keep those times free from ministry talk. Whether we go out to dinner, a movie, or take a walk on the beach, we try to focus on each other and not on our ministry. Making time for ourselves has been a challenge, but one that we have learned is extremely important for our family and our ministry.

The other difficulty is when the stress at home carries over to work or vice versa. It is very difficult to run a youth group meeting together after yelling at each other only minutes before.

Question:

Do you ever feel in competition with Steve?

Lisa:

It feels great to be able to say "No" to that question. For many years, I felt like I was competing with Steve. I felt I needed his personality and his gifts to do effective ministry. But as I have developed my own gifts, we have begun to complement each other naturally. Knowing what my gifts are and having confidence in myself have been key factors in us being able to minister as codirectors.

Question:

Besides knowing your own gifts, what tips would you give to women who work side by side with their husbands in youth ministry?

Lisa:

1. Never compare yourself with your husband.
2. Give him his space at work and at home.
3. Do not criticize him in front of others.
4. Take time to affirm his gifts. Let him do the same for you.
5. Schedule a time when you specifically communicate about

the needs of the ministry for that week.
6. Pray together.
7. Always put family before ministry.
8. Take a day off.
9. And finally, remember the ministry is not yours or his but the Lord's.

ADVENTURE NUMBER THREE
Ministry as a Married Woman with a Husband Not Directly Involved in Youth Ministry: Helen Musick

Early in Helen Musick's marriage she approached her husband, John, with what she thought was a fantastic idea. "John, let's do youth ministry together! We'll have a great time and you'll love it."

In Helen's own words, "Boy, was I wrong. It was a disaster. John did *not* enjoy youth ministry." It was at that point Helen knew her own call to youth ministry would not be shared with her husband. She recalls, "He gave it his best try but it ended up draining him instead of energizing him."

The opposite is true for Helen. Her love for youth ministry has grown during her 17 years of academic and ministry experience. She received her B.S. in Elementary Education from the University of Tennessee, her M.A. in Religious Education from Asbury Seminary, and is currently pursuing further graduate work in Family Studies (Adolescent Development) at the University of Kentucky. Her academic studies have been enhanced by her past ministry experiences as a Young Life volunteer and church youth pastor, as well as her current position as an instructor of youth ministry at Asbury Seminary. Helen understands all too well the difficulties and victories of serving in a youth ministry with a husband who is not directly involved.

Question:
Helen, what is the number one advantage of being in youth ministry without your husband?

Helen:

I feel a sense of freedom to express myself as an individual and to excel and develop the gifts of my own individuality.

Question:

On the flip side, what is the most difficult aspect of being involved in a ministry without John?

Helen:

Interestingly, what I enjoy most about my situation is also the greatest difficulty. While I am able to have my own niche to develop in ministry, I miss being able to share the joy of joint ministry. John likes teenagers; he just doesn't seem to possess the vision and innate ability to minister to them.

Question:

How does your husband respond to your busy schedule as a professor and youth worker?

Helen:

I try to do much of my ministry during the day when he's at work. Or, I spend time with students on nights when he has meetings or commitments. Of course, there are times when I need to be away, but he seems to enjoy the time he has with our children.

Question:

Does he resent your schedule?

Helen:

No, he doesn't. At times my youth events and teaching responsibilities mean that he has to shoulder more work around the house. But because we discuss my ministry responsibilities and I involve him in the decision process, he doesn't resent my schedule.

Question:

What about the idea that the ideal marriage is one in which the husband and wife share the same calling?

Helen:

I don't buy it, at least for us. And I don't see it in Scripture. John is completely supportive of my calling and sends me off with his blessing. He verbally expresses his support and even a sense of pride in my ministry and accomplishments. If I ministered without his blessing, I would wonder whether or not I should actually be in youth ministry.

Question:

How about spiritual leadership in your home?

Helen:

John and I are equally yoked; we are both spiritually on the same level. Our marriage is based upon servanthood. Jesus clearly emphasizes that spirituality expresses itself in servanthood. I do look to John for a sense of leadership in our home. The respect that I choose to give him seems to bring balance and wholeness in our relationship.

Question:

Besides servanthood in your marriage, what other tips would you give to women who serve in youth ministry while their husbands don't?

Helen:

Remember what's important: God first, husband second, children third, and ministry fourth. Make sure your church leadership also understands your calling as a wife, mother, and youth pastor. With your husband, establish clear guidelines for yourself about time off and nights out. Protect yourself. Protect your family. Be the best wife and mother you can be and your ministry will be all the better for it.

ADVENTURE NUMBER FOUR
Ministry as a Mother: Jean Tippit

Can a woman do it all? Can a woman be an effective youth worker, have a fulfilling marriage, and be a committed mom? It's tough, but it can be done.

Just ask Jean Tippit. Since 1987, she has been the full-time Director of Youth at Christ United Methodist Church in Mobile, Alabama. Her husband, Keith, owns his own teleproduction studio. Their three-year-old daughter, Amy, is one of her greatest delights.

Question:
How has your ministry perspective changed after becoming a mother?

Jean:
My relationships with our students' parents, especially mothers, have deepened. Somehow having a child has helped me relate more on the mothers' level. I now have a better understanding of how or why parents make certain decisions, and I can help students understand their view.

Question:
How do your students respond to Amy?

Jean:
They love her! She introduces herself and me to just about everyone. She attracts kids to her at schools, stores, ballgames, wherever. She's like a magnet.

Question:
Are you ever worried that Amy might feel neglected because of your devotion to your ministry?

Jean:
No, I'm not. I continually pray that God will help me keep my priorities straight. Plus my husband, Keith, keeps me balanced. Keith is my rock, my strength. I know that he wants the best for me and for our family.

One thing that we are very careful about is that we don't want Amy to be "overchurched." Keith and I try to take her to church the same amount as an average family. In fact, at times Keith stays home with her to help Amy maintain this balance.

Question:
What do you do about youth ministry overnighters and trips? Do you take Amy with you?

Jean:
It's a tough call but I try to evaluate it by asking myself four questions. First, will I be able to supervise my own child? I don't want our youth or volunteers to feel like I am dumping Amy on them. Second, will I be able to minister effectively? I want to be at my best and give my students the attention they deserve. Sometimes, my students need just me. Third, if I leave Amy behind, will I have peace of mind and be able to concentrate on the ministry event? If I leave her behind, but continue to worry about her, I'm only giving part of myself to the students. And finally, will I, will Amy, and will my students enjoy the event? Sometimes Amy doesn't want to go; sometimes I don't want her to go, and sometimes I just have to make a decision and pray that it is the correct one.

Question:
What are some of the important lessons that being a mother in ministry has taught you?

Jean:
My own child comes first. She needs that, the Bible commands it, and my church and youth group understand that.

Second, I can never give up ministry. There is no reason that I or any other mother cannot do ministry. I often think of Philippians 4:13, "I can do everything through Christ who strengthens me." To me, this means I can do youth ministry as well as be a wife and a mom as Christ gives me the strength. Every woman is different and has to evaluate her own unique situation, but for me I wouldn't have it any other way.

ADVENTURE NUMBER FIVE
Ministry as a Wife of a Youth Pastor:
Eilleen Rollerson

"See this fishbowl. This is your life."

Eilleen Rollerson remembers these rather ominous words, spoken at a workshop for ministers' wives several years ago. Her husband, Derrick, is one of the two full-time youth pastors at Westlawn Gospel Chapel in Illinois. Their three children, coupled with Eilleen's volunteer involvement with her husband's youth ministry and various Christian organizations, keep Eilleen on the cutting edge of the needs of youth workers' wives.

Question:

What is your favorite aspect of volunteering alongside your husband?

Eilleen:

It allows me to be with my husband doing what we both like best, namely "kingdom building." Plus, unlike my husband, I have the freedom to choose the projects I'd like to get involved with. I share his call, but I don't believe that I need to do all that he does just because I'm his wife.

Question:

Eilleen, do you really have freedom to choose what you want to do, or do you feel the weight of others' expectations for you to be involved in everything as a pastor's wife?

Eilleen:

Although the way others see me is important to me, I try not to let those thoughts dictate my actions. I realized early in my Christian life and ministry that others might have unrealistic expectations of me. The younger women seemed to expect my behaviors to be supernaturally holy, while the older ones seemed to look for mistakes. My freedom to be myself has come from the balance between respecting others while yet maintaining a sense of my own identity and needs.

Question:
What highlight stands out in your marriage and ministry?

Eilleen:
God has repeatedly confirmed His promises to us. In past years, He provided even at times when we didn't have food or money, and there was no paycheck in sight. One morning in particular, we had been married for a few years, when Derrick informed me that he had invited a couple over for dinner that evening. I was furious and embarrassed because I knew there was nothing to eat and we had no money. I angrily asked him what we were supposed to feed them. He responded, ''Where's your faith?''

I asked him what he suggested I try to serve that night. He asked me to prepare meatloaf, cabbage, mashed potatoes, and cornbread. Then he suggested we pray and turn our dilemma over to the Lord.

Later that day, we visited my husband's parents. As we were leaving their home, his mom remembered a gift she had set aside for us. Into the basement she went, only to return with a package of frozen ground beef, a five pound bag of potatoes, a large head of cabbage, and a box of corn muffin mix. They were the complete ingredients for the meal that Derrick and I had prayed about that very morning! This is only one example of the exciting testimony we have of God's faithfulness.

Question:
Do you ever feel like you and your family come after your husband's ministry?

Eilleen:
Confess that at times I become envious of the amount of time that he spends doing ministry work. The key for us is to find creative ways to purposefully set aside time for each other — at least a few hours each week. Plus when I'm under stress at home, Derrick tries to come home between meetings or rearrange his schedule to allow me to rest or have some personal time alone. We both believe our marriage and our children need to come before the ministry.

Question:
We all face times when the load of ministry and our families seems heavy. What keeps you going?

Eilleen:
My husband and I, as well as every follower of Jesus Christ, have the awesome responsibility of spreading the Gospel to the lost. The Lord has a master plan. We are soldiers following His leading. Derrick and I have vowed that our goal together is to strive to please the Lord so that when we will stand before Him, we will hear "well done."

CONCLUSION

The journeys may look different, but the goal is the same: to point teenagers toward God. May we also always have the secondary goal of enjoying the adventure.

BARRIER BREAKERS

1. What does your journey look like right now?

2. What are the important lessons this journey is teaching you?

3. What are some of the joys that you find in the midst of your adventures?

4. What do you believe God is calling you to do as your next step?

SIX

Search for the Right Fit
Finding out who you are and how you minister

by Rick Dunn and Jana Sundene

'm just not sure where God is calling me to minister."
"I don't know what type of ministry I should be looking
for."

"How do I know God's will?"

"How do I know what type of ministry I will be good at?"

As professors and leadership partners in the youth ministry department of a Christian college, we encounter these comments from students on a weekly basis. What a privilege it is to be able to walk alongside these young men and women during critical passages in their ministry journey. Along with our sense of privilege, however, comes the awareness of the responsibility for guiding students, not simply toward positions of service, but towards the One whom they desire to serve.

The following ideas, examples, and methods represent the steps we use to assist students, lay workers, and youth ministry professionals as they seek to answer the questions above. Combining more than 30 years of youth ministry leadership experience and our different personalities and ministry giftedness, we will describe the key issues a person must address when considering a place for ministry leadership. More specifically, we will present how we respond to students and graduates as they try to find their best ministry fit.

Before we get to the "how to's" of finding the right fit, we want you to consider why we take the approach we do. The *why* is summarized in the following foundational beliefs:

1. The primary consideration in choosing a ministry position is for the leader to better be able to experience, ex-

press, and explore a loving relationship with God.
Gwyn Baker, a youth ministry veteran of twenty-five years, recently challenged our senior students to remember, "Our first call is to love God, not students. We must love students out of our love for God." We are, therefore, convinced that God must be the beginning and end of our discernment process if we desire Him to be the goal of our ministry service.

A "God-ward" perspective is critical if we are to journey obediently toward a place of ministry leadership. We must avoid ever focusing *primarily* on the task of choosing a *place* to minister. Such a misdirected focus can leave us frustrated, anxious, and even angry when we do not "get an answer" immediately from God! God's first call for us is to know Him and to love Him above all else. It is through the knowing and loving of who He is that we begin to experience His specific will for our lives. It is this passionate love for God that then leads us to follow Him in His will for our lives. If we reverse that order, we will find ourselves being servants who have forgotten to be children.

2. God is at work in every person's life to glorify Himself in a unique manner.
There is no magic formula for identifying where a person should be involved in ministry. There exists no one personality test, spiritual gift inventory, leadership seminar, or chapter in a youth ministry text, which will be *the key* for everyone. Each of us has a special way to bring honor to His name and provide service to His kingdom.

3. Calling supersedes location.
We are committed to our calling to invest in the women and men God is raising up for the next generation of youth ministry leadership around the world. For example, if our college fired us both tomorrow, our "ministry" would not be over. Ministering is not what we do, it's *who* we are. Our ministry would continue in another form in another place because it is who we are and what we have been called to do. Too often youth workers confuse calling with location. Rather, calling is the persistent, progressive work of God in one's life which, over a lifetime of service, might manifest itself in a variety of positions in a variety of locations.

4. Youth ministry leadership will be both a place to nurture and to be nurtured.

Youth ministry positions need to be chosen not just for how one can minister, but for how we can be ministered to. In other words, ministry contexts should be places in which we find ourselves in mentoring relationships and/or community experiences which deepen our personal spiritual maturity, as well as a place to minister to others. For far too long, youth ministry leadership has been seen as a place where people give "110 percent," crash and burn, then move on to something else. We need to be committed to long-term ministry, not just short-term service. Some of the most effective ministry is accomplished by seasoned veterans who have found balance and wisdom over time.

LOOKING AT MINISTRY THROUGH YOUR PERSONAL WINDOW

Given the previous beliefs, it will become apparent why our discernment process begins and ends with examining one's personal relationship with God. Our department's founding slogan is, "Before God builds a youth ministry, He builds a youth minister." With this in mind, we challenge students to approach a ministry position as a place to invest who they have been created to be, who they are presently becoming, and who they perceive they have been called to be in the future.

To accomplish this end, we ask students to examine youth ministry opportunities from the viewpoint of a "Personal Window." Looking through this window, they can begin to evaluate particular ministry settings and discern which one is a good fit.

Pane #1: Growth Process
All of my (Rick's) relatives live south of the Mason-Dixon line. When I plan a trip to visit family members, I have to check a road map, prepare the vehicle, and gather supplies for the drive. During the actual driving, however, I focus my attention fully on what I see just ahead of the vehicle. I occasionally glance towards the horizon, but safe driving demands that I see and adjust to what lies just ahead.

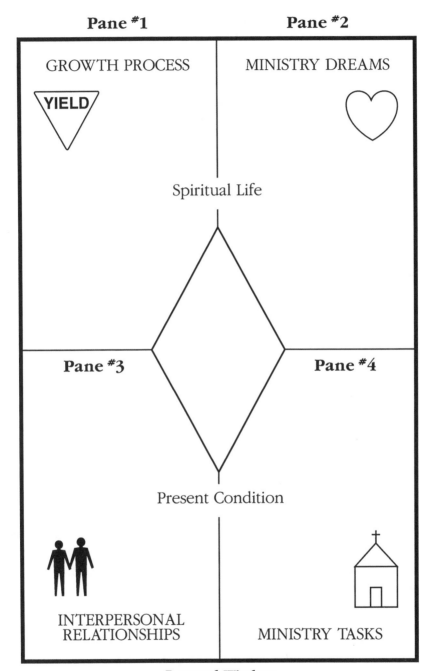

Personal Window

When pursuing and evaluating ministry options, it is critical to focus on one's immediate personal journey. Questions to ask yourself include:

- What lies just ahead for me in my growth?
- Is the next portion of my "growth trip" a time when I need to work on my struggles with anger?
- Is there some "personal baggage" hindering my journey?
- Is there a new skill (conflict management, empathic listening, etc.) that I should be working on?

In light of the anticipated growth process which lies ahead, what type of relational environment do I need to facilitate that growth? What type of ministry tasks are congruent with where I am and where I need to be?

Pane #2: Ministry Dreams

ESPN recently began an advertising campaign centering on the slogan: "It could happen." In their commercials, athletes describe their "ESPN Fantasy." Big, lumbering linemen score touchdowns on graceful runs and ordinary athletes make extraordinary heroic plays followed by the words, "It could happen."

Dreaming is critical to expanding your ministry horizon. Dreaming also provides clues to the ministry calling and passion God has placed within each of us.

Too much ministry is done with a sense of obligation rather than vision. Vision requires dreaming and allows God's Word and Spirit to build our passion. Keeping in touch with your visions and dreams is vital for choosing an appropriate ministry situation. Be careful not to limit God with predetermined ideas. Be open to exploring new ways and new places where your ministry dreams could come true.

- What does your ideal ministry look like?
- What energizes you as you think about ministry?
- If anything was possible, even your wildest dream, and success was guaranteed, what would you do?

IT COULD HAPPEN!

Pane #3: Interpersonal Relationships

Every person differs in the ways in which he or she is able to initiate, sustain, and deepen interpersonal relationships. Because ministry consists of relationships and not just programs, we must be aware of our relational abilities, styles, and tendencies.

We, Jana and Rick, are very different in our relational styles. Jana is quieter, more reserved, and develops strong, loyal relationships with a few people over a long period of time. Rick, on the other hand, initiates multiple relationships, and has a large network of friends and colleagues. As a result, we have not only been able to complement, but also sharpen one another. Without an understanding of our communication styles, we would be frustrated and disappointed with each other. Instead, we can rejoice in our differences and benefit from our diversity.

Authentic self-discovery requires receiving feedback from significant others. In addition, you can facilitate self-discovery through the use of instruments such as, the DISC (personal profile) by Performax, the Kiersey Temperament Sorter, and spiritual gift discernment courses/seminars.

- With whom are you most likely to build relationships?
- With whom do you experience the most difficulty communicating?
- When do you feel most comfortable: in a crowd, a small group, or one-on-one?
- Do you most enjoy young children, junior highers, senior highers, or college students?
- How do you handle conflict and confrontation?
- How do you like to work on tasks: with a group, by yourself, or in a closely knit team?
- With whom do you work best?
- What type of relationships energize or deplete you?

Pane #4: Ministry Tasks

God has gifted the body of Christ so that different people contribute to the whole. We, Jana and Rick, are very different in our contributions. Rick is a big-picture, vision developer and visioncaster. Rick is able to motivate and lead people toward increased commitment and personal growth. Jana is gifted with the ability to map out a detailed step-by-step process necessary to bring a vision to reality. Jana is able to see that the steps are followed through, offering detailed guidance as people progress through the process. Combined, these gifts complement one another.

- In light of your past and present ministry relationships, what do you do best?
  - What energizes you in ministry?
  - What builds your passion?
  - What things frustrate you in ministry?
  - What is your unique contribution?
  - How is your contribution like or unlike others?
  - What have you been affirmed for in the past?

Spiritual Life

All of these panes in the personal window point back to understanding ourselves as God created, redeemed, and is now nurturing us for His glory. Where are you presently in your journey with God? Looking through the four panes of the personal window, how is God at work in you? What response is He calling you to?

Two key ideas related to your spiritual life should be stressed as you walk through the above processes of self-discovery. First, *celebrate.* Rejoice in who God has made you to be. It is so easy to want to be able to sing like that person, to speak to a group like someone else, and to have small group leadership skills like yet another. Too often we forget to celebrate our own unique giftedness which God has designed for His body. Second, *cultivate.* KEEP ON GROWING! Flex and use your strong muscles while finding ways to develop your weak areas.

Discerning a ministry position should not be a panic-filled experience. Rather, it should be a natural progression of the journey God has begun in you. "Faithful is He who calls you, and He also will bring it to pass" (1 Thes. 5:24, NASB).

A Clear Focus

The personal window is designed to move us all past shortsightedness and the urgency of the moment. In addition, our personal self-discovery and our renewed vision for God's will in our lives provides a lens to help us clearly see the appropriateness of a ministry opportunity. We can't let fear limit the possibilities, nor narrow our potential.

ARTICULATING YOUR UNIQUE CONTRIBUTION

Once you have taken some time to discover what gifts, passion, and strengths you bring to a ministry, practice clearly articulating your unique contribution. Whether you are entering into a ministry as a volunteer or as a "professional," you probably possess the same desire: to make a unique contribution to a worthwhile ministry. We all want to invest our lives in something significant. Learning to articulate your strengths and passions can be a benefit whether it helps you know how to choose a ministry or redefine roles within a current ministry. Here are a few important steps in clearly articulating about yourself.

1. What contribution can you make to this particular ministry?
Have you ever sat around with a group of friends trying to decide what each person could contribute to a progressive dinner? There's always someone who is famous for making cheesecake. He is the dessert stop. Someone else has a reputation for the most incredible chili. She gets assigned the main dish. And so on. Consider the questions raised by the personal window. What do *you* bring to the ministry? What's your "specialty"?

With these perspectives in mind, begin to picture yourself in this particular ministry context. What are the needs of the ministry that your gifts would meet? Who are the people in this ministry that you would be drawn to minister to? What kind of ministry could you see yourself having with those people? What types of existing roles in this ministry appeal to you? How do you envision yourself carrying out that role?

It is possible that in the ministry you are investigating there is no role that you would fit at this present time. Perhaps you could mentally *create* a role that fits you and benefits the ministry. If you can articulate your "dream role" clearly and with passion, you may find that the leadership is willing to create a place for you. If you are applying for a traditional youth pastor position, you may want to articulate how you can fulfill that role *through* what you can uniquely bring to the position.

Being creative and articulate once helped me (Jana) through a difficult ministry situation. I was about to get "dismissed" from my three-quarter-time position as an associate director who was responsible for recruiting, training, and developing volunteer staff leaders. The position was one for which I had received nothing but praise and positive feedback for the six months I had served. However, the board decided that as a churchwide trend, all paid leaders should possess as one of their top spiritual gifts the gift of leadership. Unfortunately, I didn't fit the category because my top gifts were shepherding and teaching. Sitting nervously before one of the board members, I tried to articulate exactly why a person with the gift of shepherding was the perfect fit for the position I was in. I connected the needs with my strengths and gifts. I calmly but passionately related my desire to encourage, train, and equip the leaders under my care. I left the office knowing that I had presented a straightforward picture of who I was and how I felt I could make a meaningful contribution. The result? I kept my job, and was promoted to a full-time staff position. I believe that it is important to be able to articulate who we are and what we can offer in order to find the right ministry fit. The existing leadership cannot read your mind. You must be able to accurately tell them about you.

2. Think about what kinds of contributions you are presently able to make.

I can visualize my all-time dream role in a ministry, but if I don't have the time, energy, or motivation to fulfill that role, then it is futile. We need to think through these two steps and combine the results in order to come up with a clear idea of what we are able *and willing* to contribute.

We all pass through seasons. Some seasons afford us energy to tackle major obstacles. Other seasons leave us emotionally or physically drained. Reasonably, what will you be able to contribute at this time? At what level can you be wholeheartedly involved during this season of your life? In what way could you meaningfully contribute without sabotaging yourself or overloading yourself somewhere down the line? As you create needed boundaries, you can safely express and serve, while increasing your energy, by using your God-given gifts wisely.

3. Define your philosophy of ministry and ministry statement.

Discover what your beliefs are regarding successful ministry.

Many of us have never uncovered them. Beliefs are convictions we feel strongly about. For example, beliefs might include strong feelings about what is appropriate and what's not, what is essential and what is unnecessary, and what we feel makes a ministry effective. These beliefs may be developed from our study of Scripture or from trial and error in our own experiences.

In order to define your philosophy, ask yourself some questions. These questions won't answer how you will minister. Rather, they will define the basis and priorities for ministry.

1. How do you define effective ministry?

2. What should be a youth pastor's priorities?

3. What is the most effective way to minister to the people being served?

4. What is my responsibility to the ministry?

5. How do I feel a youth minister should act?

6. How important is the leadership development of volunteers?

7. What place should the governing board hold in the ministry?

8. How important is a team concept, and how much decision-making power should the team hold?

After answering these questions, combine them in written form into a one page ministry philosophy.

From that one page document boil the contents down to a one paragraph statement defining your personal ministry statement. Although you may change ministries, your personal ministry statement will most likely remain the same.

Here's an example of a ministry statement:

> *My goal in ministry is to model Christ to students and encourage their spiritual development by helping them to integrate God's Word into their lives, through teaching and example.*

DETERMINING A GOOD FIT

1. Finding a philosophical match.

Determine if your main beliefs about ministry are compatible with the ministry of which you wish to become a part. For example, if you believe that evangelism should be a secondary goal after discipleship, then it would be contrary to your ministry philosophy to join a para-church campus ministry whose main goal is evangelism. You will spend valuable time frustrated over the philosophical differences. Beware of thinking that you will be the one to change the philosophical underpinnings of any organization! They are usually deeply held and rarely changed.

2. Look for a ministry that values who you are.

The best ministry fits are created when both you *and* the ministry leadership understand and value your potential contribution.

Does the ministry want and need a person like you? Will your "brand" of passion be appreciated? Will your types of gifts be esteemed? Will you be valued for who you are and what you can bring to the ministry? How are people communicating that they value you? Search for a place where you are valued and affirmed in your uniqueness.

3. Find a ministry that gives you opportunities to express your gifts and abilities.

Maybe you are thinking that if you find a place that values who you are, the leadership will naturally give you opportunities to express yourself. By and large, if you are genuinely valued, this will be true. Unfortunately, it is not a "given." I know of a situation where the leadership team of a ministry genuinely saw the need to add a female leader to bring balance to the ministry and to meet the unique needs of the female volunteer staff. But once they made her a part of the team, she wasn't given any real opportunity to add her perspective or to meet the needs that she saw. She was limited to meeting the needs *they* perceived in the ways *they* felt were best. I also know of a guy who was being pursued for a ministry position because of his entrepreneurial abilities, but discovered during the interview process that the church had a distinct way they wanted him to run the ministry, not allowing him the opportunity to express the very quality they were seeking after. Ask yourself, *will this ministry or lead-*

ership team allow me opportunities to use the gifts and abilities and express the passion I bring to it?

4. Find a ministry that allows you to personally grow and expand as a child of God.

Your growth and nurture should be a priority of the organization. If you are not being ministered to, it won't be long before you experience burnout, stagnation, apathy, or disillusionment. Search for an environment which allows for your growth as a person and as a Christian. Investigate to find a ministry flexible enough to allow you to adjust your role as you discover more about who you are. Will the ministry provide resources to strengthen your weak areas? Does this ministry offer personal support and allow you room to develop individual support networks?

Ministries to avoid are ones that are so performance based that they do not allow you to be in process as a person, leader, and Christian. We have met some very tired leaders who are worn out from trying to portray the picture perfect leader they thought they were expected to be. They are stagnant in their Christian walk because they were not allowed to have doubts or ask questions (for fear of looking like they are not "all together") which could have been the catalyst to take them to their next level of growth. And we have known too many burned out volunteers who used to love working with youth, but because of poor ministry situations have vowed to never volunteer again. The problem? The ministry used their gifts and talents but neglected to offer any kind of nurture or support along the way. Look for a ministry which offers you encouragement along the way. One that values people over performance.

Seeking a Place of Obedience (Not Perfection)
Although no ministry is perfect, we have tried to point out a basic blueprint which we believe will help you find the most optimal place to minister. However, ministries (like people) are in process. The key is to find the best fit possible. But don't expect perfection. I (Jana) know that in my four separate contexts of ministry, I have not found any situation which scores a perfect ten. Depend on the Holy Spirit to lead you as He illuminates each step of your way.

BARRIER BREAKERS

1. Give yourself time to reflectively work through the issues presented in this chapter. Share the results, including your Personal Window, with a mentor or peer who could provide feedback on your perspectives.

2. Spend some time developing or sharpening your philosophy of ministry.

3. Write a page or two that clearly articulates what you think your unique contribution to ministry is. If you are currently in a ministry, take time to communicate this to those with whom you work most closely.

4. Use the criteria for finding a right fit as an outline to evaluate your present situation or one you are considering becoming a part of.

Authors

Name: *Jana Sundene*

Occupation: *Professor of Youth Ministry at Trinity International University and College of Liberal Arts in Deerfield, Illinois*
Birthplace: *Chicago*
Current home: *Buffalo Grove, Illinois*
My favorite food is: *Shrimp*
The last movie that significantly impacted me was: The Shawshank Redemption
The style that best reflects me is: *Simple, natural*
Favorite childhood memory is: *Playing in the fields and pond by my house and making forts*
A good book that I would recommend is: Chicken Soup for the Soul
I've never been able to: *Say entrepreneur*
Nobody knows I'm: *shy*
I'd give anything to meet: *Frances Farmer (she's dead) or Margaret Becker*
If I could change one thing about myself: *I'd be more* naturally *friendly and sociable*
If I weren't in youth ministry, I'd be: *A professor (just kidding), an architect, phone repair person, speaker/author*
I love to: *Travel the world*
I really don't care for: *Potato salad*
My favorite pet is: *My dog Lindsey!*
It really bugs me when: *People hang their wet towels over my dry ones*
The thing that I love about youth ministry is: *The potential contained in the young*
My favorite place to spend time with God is: *In the mountains or at the ocean at night*
I would like to be remembered for: *Encouraging and developing the potential of others*

Name: *Rick Dunn*

Occupation: *Professor of Christian Education and Youth Ministry at Trinity International University and College of Liberal Arts in Deerfield, Illinois*
Birthplace: *Cleveland, Tennessee*
My favorite food is: *Ice cream*
The style that best reflects me is: *Casual*
Favorite childhood memory is: *In the mountains of eastern Tennessee*

A good book that I would recommend is: *A Long Obedience in the Same Direction by Eugene Peterson*
I've never been able to: *Dunk a basketball with two hands*
If I could change one thing about myself: *I'd be more organized*
If I weren't in youth ministry, I'd be: *Coaching high school basketball*
I love to: *Play with my kids and be with my family*
People always think I'm: *An extrovert, but I'm really an introvert*
I really don't care for: *Stuffy, structured, dull, and boring environments*
The thing that I love about youth ministry is: *Being a part of a long-term investment in changing a person's life*
My favorite place to spend time with God is: *The mountains*
I would like to be remembered for: *Integrity and authenticity in relationships*
If there is one thing that I would like to tell my colleagues, it would be: *Cultivate the internal, and the external will take care of itself*

SEVEN

Barriers along the Way

*Understanding and overcoming the obstacles
women face*

by Ginny Olson

I came around the corner of the old Jewish quarter. "There it
is!" exclaimed a fellow pilgrim.

My eyes searched frantically, trying to find the spot
amidst the yellow stone. "Where?"

"Look down, to the lower left."

Ah, of course. Now I recognized it. The sight I remembered
from grade school documentaries. The place where Jews gathered from around the world, the reminder of the temple that
once was.

Already, the trip had been one of overwhelming emotions
and experiences. Turning a bend in the road meant coming
face-to-face with a familiar story. "That mountain on the
left . . . that's where Elijah dealt with the prophets of Baal."
"See those caves in those hills to the south of us? That's where
the demoniac existed until Jesus healed him."

This was a trek I had been planning for ten months. It was
one I had dreamed of for years. I was with eighteen fellow pilgrims — people traveling not as tourists seeing "The Holy Land"
but people searching for God in the midst of history.

As our group walked down the ramp to the square, a guide
explained to us that the Wall is an active synagogue. This meant
that the men and women cannot worship together. In an active
synagogue, they are separated by some type of a barrier, be it a
clumsily hung sheet or, in this case, yards of waist-high fencing.

I stood in the square, surveying all that was going on, trying to absorb it into my memory. The place was animated. I
watched the men as they disappeared into one of the cavernous

entrances on the side wall, appearing seconds later with their heads covered, in the closed off area in front of the Wall. Off to the right, the women gathered at the women's section of the Wall, outside the barrier. There were women in heavy winter raincoats with faded scarves tied over graying hair. Others were in jean jackets and Birkenstocks. Some stood in line, waiting for a chance to place a hand on the ancient stones while saying their prayers. Fingers carefully tucked prayers in the crevices of the stone wall. Others sat back a few yards in school chairs, gently rocking back and forth as they prayed.

Today the majority of the women gathered around the waist-high fences surrounding the men's section. It was Bar Mitzvah day and their sons, nephews, and brothers were being honored in their passage into manhood. From the sidelines, women leaned over the fence and screamed and cheered. They threw bright pieces of candy in celebration as the men gathered around the boys, solemn in their prayer shawls and yarmulkes.

I moved into line to wait for my turn at the wall while watching the excitement to my left. Oblivious to the commotion, the swallows darted in and out of an outcropping of vines, just above the heads of the women bowed in prayer.

As I finally took my turn in front of the famous wall, my fingers feeling the worn corners of stones, I began to cry. The separateness of the men and women overwhelmed me. This is the way it had been for centuries. This is where Mary had been taught the truths from Scripture — from the outer court. This is where women had been relegated throughout history . . . off to the side, behind a curtain, beyond a barrier.

I thought of the women in ministry I have known who have been ostracized by similar barriers. Women who have had to reign in their strength and leadership because they did not fit in an orthodox system. Women who have struggled with their role and call in ministry because they were told that they had to be submissive and compliant. Women who didn't believe they could actually minister beyond Vacation Bible School.

Facing the cracks stuffed with tiny papers, a verse kept quietly running through the midst of my chaotic thoughts. Doesn't the Bible say that "in Christ there is no Jew or Greek . . . no male or female"? I was overwhelmed as I began to comprehend the freedom we have in Christ AS WOMEN.

I'm not trying to make a statement on the rightness or wrongness of what was happening at the Wall. It just is and has been and will be for a long time. Rather, I was reminded again that even if we don't face physical barriers today, we still encounter emotional ones, born of tradition. Some of these barriers we have even erected ourselves. These are barriers that keep us from learning about who God is, how He has created us to serve Him in joy—barriers that keep us from fully using our gifts and our weaknesses, to glorify Him.[1]

In this chapter, I want to look at some of the barriers women face in youth ministry today, both from the inside and the outside.

A word of caution before we begin: these barriers can come with emotional explosives attached. Barriers aren't neutral. They wouldn't be barriers if they weren't keeping us from something we wanted. By their very nature, some of these will be covered with controversy. Listen to your "gut" as you explore them. If your anger rises to the surface, where does it come from? Apathetic—why? Surprise—what haven't you had to deal with . . . yet?

Some male leaders may have experienced these barriers as well. They are not always based on gender. In my time in youth ministry, I have found many men who are committed to breaking down barriers for women. They are strong advocates for partnership in our quest to communicate God's love to students. In examining these barriers, it is my hope that we can begin to dismantle them or at least turn them into speed bumps.

THE BARRIER OF DISCOURAGEMENT

One of the most puzzling barriers we face is the reaction to our ministry of those closest to us. It's puzzling because we hope and even expect that those who surround us will be supportive of our choice to be in youth ministry. It's discouraging to have well-meaning friends, family members, church members, and even senior pastors question the validity of our being in ministry. These people can be subtle—not asking any questions about our ministry, hoping if they ignore it long enough, it will go away. They can also be blatant, sometimes to the point of being cruel — cutting off communication with us because they disagree with ministry as a career choice. These people can question our being in ministry because of a theological disagreement "women shouldn't be in leadership in ministry" or because they don't think youth ministry is a valid career. Which of us hasn't been asked the question, "No, really. What are you going to do when you grow up?"

At a national youth ministry conference a young woman, bubbling with excitement stopped me in the hotel lobby. We had both been part of a seminar that focused on dreaming and discussing the current and future state of women in youth ministry. "I never understood before this weekend that women could be youth pastors. This has been a dream of mine for a long time. My husband and I are going to be praying about a place where we can serve as a team in youth ministry." Then she lowered her voice and furrowed her brow as she continued. "I was sitting at lunch with a group from our denomination. I was so excited as I talked about my new dreams. Suddenly, I realized that no one was smiling or nodding or giving me any signs of affirmation except my husband. Now I understand what you and the other women who have been in youth ministry have had to go through."

Surprisingly, those who can be the biggest discouragers are other women. In the famous and overused words of Walt Kelly's cartoon character Pogo, "We have met the enemy . . . and they is us." Sometimes this discouragement is rooted in legitimate differences of theological belief, although I've known several women with whom I've disagreed theologically, and they did not discourage me. We agreed to disagree. Usually, if other women are negative about ministry involvement, the roots of this negativity can be traced to something else, such as competition and jealousy. Some women who have been raised to believe women can only fit in certain boxes are threatened when they see others refusing to fit into those same boxes. They watch other women doing what they have secretly dreamed of and, almost on an unconscious level, sabotage their success. I interviewed a woman once who sat in a church meeting and had a mother of one of her students stand up and say, "We need a man as the youth pastor." The mother's reasoning was that she had a male youth pastor when she was a teenager, and her child needed that as well. The youth pastor became a victim of church-wide groupthink and quickly found herself out of a job.

Other church staff can also be discouragers. One youth worker was still in the honeymoon phase of her new youth pastorate when the senior pastor pulled her aside and said, "I didn't want you to get this job." His remark came as a complete shock to her. Until then, she had been looking forward to their working together. It turned out that he had a friend whom he had wanted to hire but was unable to. He proceeded to make her job miserable. A few years later, frustrated and discouraged, she left the job that the pastor had never wanted her to have in the first place.

The fact is that there aren't many women who have chosen to be in youth ministry, and those who have are pioneers. A pioneer is someone who explores and faces new territory. Many times the terrain is difficult and the path barely distinguishable. However, although pioneers face tough and discouraging times, they forge ahead, knowing that their journey is not for themselves alone, but for the many that will one day follow.

One way to break through this barrier of discouragement is to surround yourself with people who affirm your call into youth ministry. Who do you have that you can go to when you smack into this barrier? You need to have a few people in your life that you can call at any hour who will remind you why you got into youth ministry in the first place.

Another idea to fight discouragement is to keep a "feel good" file. This is a place where you save cards and letters that you've received in ministry from students and their parents. When you enter the "slough of despondency," pull out your file and remind yourself that there are people out there who believe in you and in your ability to be a minister.

And yet another way to break through this barrier is to spend time writing down why you believe God called you to minister to students. Incorporate the Scripture passages He used to affirm this call. Refer back to this record when the voices of discouragement grow loud.

THE BARRIER OF LIMITED OPPORTUNITIES

I was having lunch with several people in youth ministry. The person on my right was a Christian Education professor. I knew several women who were his students and were grateful for his support of their pursuits. The lunchtime conversation turned to the status of professional women in youth ministry. The professor posed a rhetorical question in a bewildered voice, "When a woman is spending $25,000 on a college education, how can I advise her to go into a field where I'm not sure she can get a job?" Part of me was frustrated that a question like that could be asked in this day, and yet another part of me knew there was a large kernel of truth in that question.

One of the reasons Diane Elliot and I formed Journey was that we were hearing both sides of a Catch-22. We were becoming aware of ministries that were searching for qualified women for paid youth ministry positions. We were also talking to college women who had a heart for youth ministry, yet were not considering it as a career because they didn't know any female youth pastors and thus assumed there were no jobs for women in this field. This erroneous assumption was costing youth ministry gifted and passionate workers.

Is it really more difficult for a woman to find a youth ministry position than for a man? If you're looking at only conservative evangelical churches, then the answer is yes, it is more difficult, but not impossible. As more churches are opening up to women in leadership, more jobs are surfacing as well. Churches are seeing the importance of having their students be exposed to both male and female leaders.

When looking for a position in youth ministry, women need to be open to alternatives beyond the church. Para-church organizations have historically been more open to women in leadership. Youth for Christ and Campus Crusade for Christ have had women involved in student ministry for decades. Some women have started their own ministries when they couldn't find one that was doing what they felt needed to be done in their community.

When facing the barrier of limited opportunities, women need to be flexible and creative. It may mean that in order to find a position, you need to move to another part of the country, or work part-time with a goal of the job becoming full-time at a later time. It may mean volunteering until a position opens up.

With this barrier, you also must be aware when opportunities are not going to open up, no matter how hard you try. Some churches will not change their view on women in leadership in your lifetime. Others will only see women taking on limited responsibilities. I was once an associate director for four years at a church, and also spent one year there as an interim director. When the position of director opened up, I was told that although I was qualified, those making the decision didn't believe that a woman should be a director. After five years, I knew there would be no further opportunities for me to grow at that church. It was time to move on. I went on to graduate school and further prepared myself for additional opportunities. I later moved to a church that did value women in leadership.

I've also seen some great possibilities open up and women back away because they were afraid to grab them. One reason opportunities are so exciting is because they also carry a degree of risk. What if someone asked you to speak at a camp, but you are not comfortable in front of a group of students? Some of us just naturally prefer to stay in the background. But sometimes we have to realize that in order to do what God calls us to do, we must be uncomfortable and take some risks. Is it less risky to pass up a speaking opportunity? Absolutely. You don't fail if you don't try. But you don't succeed either. And the loss is that students don't get to experience a woman being in a visible leadership position. In schools, both boys and girls are being taught that women can do anything they put their minds to. Yet, when it comes to the church, many women feel they need to check their God-given gifts (and personalities) at the door. If God opens up an opportunity to stretch, take it. Put yourself into a risky situation. Grow. Do it for the students in the audience who need to see what a godly woman looks like in leadership. They see plenty of ungodly ones throughout the week. Offer a strong alternative. Follow Esther's example. She sure wasn't comfortable in what she was called to do. But she did it anyway, putting personal fear aside. Maybe God has called *you* to this situation for such a time as this.

Let me add a challenge to the men who are reading this. You need to be asking yourself how you can open up opportunities for your female colaborers. Has God placed you in a situation where you can facilitate occasions for women to step into leadership? I am extremely grateful for the men I have encountered in ministry — some who have been my supervisors, others who have been my mentors — who have opened ministry doors for me and have guided me professionally. If the kingdom of God is to increase, we must work together. It's not just a nice idea; it's a necessity.

THE BARRIER OF THEOLOGY

Perhaps a better (but more cumbersome) heading for this section would be **The Barrier of a Poorly Thought-Out Belief System.** Let me explain.

I recently had lunch with a woman who has a strong desire to work in some capacity with students. She already has a raft of experience in the field, having organized not only local church events but also area-wide ones. She is intelligent, articulate, and well-organized. When I asked her if she was seeking a position as a youth pastor (technically, that was the job she had already been doing), her response was one I have heard many times, "Oh no. I don't want to be the one in charge." My next question was aimed to find out if this was a temperament preference or a theological view. She sat back and thought for a minute before she slowly said, "I *guess* it's a theological one."

I don't have a problem with someone saying the position she takes is a theological one, as long as she has carefully thought it through. But too often, this is used as an excuse because it's a comfortable one. Somewhere we've gotten the idea that if we wave our theological wand, it means that nobody can question our thinking. It's kind of like saying, "God told me to do this." Who's going to question God?

My response to this is that by not doing our own theological exploration, we allow someone else to do our thinking and, thus, our decision making. Ultimately, we alone are responsible for our theological slothfulness. It would have been easy for Priscilla to have kept silent and not instructed Apollos, saying that her theology wouldn't let her. Instead, she knew that God had equipped her to guide others and, in responding to this knowledge, she was a source of encouragement to the church (Acts 18). When all is said and done, we stand as individuals accountable to God. We cannot lean on senior pastors, husbands, fathers, or Christian radio pastors. We must know why we believe what we believe. And we must understand the ramifications of our belief system.

Too often women refuse to delve deeply into this issue because they fear that if they question what they have always believed, they may no longer fit into their church or ministry. Their view is that it is better to live in ignorance than in educated freedom. Just because you may come to a conclusion that is different than your church, you don't have to leave. Sometimes you may choose to stay and put your beliefs aside for the good of the church body as a whole.

This search needs to be done, no matter what your stance is. In order to break through this barrier of theology, we must look at it from all sides, even the sides with which we disagree. It is only then that we can begin to have thoughtful discussion on the topic and be quiet revolutionaries of change.

THE BARRIER OF FEAR

In our North American culture, we have (in a gross generalization) been socialized as women to view a strong personality as negatively masculine. You are, perhaps, familiar with the harsh maxim, "What's viewed as strength in a man is viewed as bitchiness in a woman." I remember trying to deal with the governing board of one ministry with which I was involved. I was hearing some rumors from "credible sources" that gross pay inequity was going on. In our department, compensation was being based on gender and marital status rather than qualifications and seniority. As I tried to pursue this through the proper channels, I finally was told, "Listen, I know you and understand you, but if this gets to the board, you'll be viewed as a. . . ." The word was never spoken but the warning was clear.

"Back off this issue. Your reputation is at stake." Being young in ministry, I backed off. I was concerned about what a potential conflict would do to the students in our ministry.

What was interesting about this situation was that it was my mother who pushed me forward to confront the problem (and she doesn't even believe women should be in key leadership roles in ministry!). But the advice she gave has stayed with me, "You are not just fighting for yourself. You need to think of the women who will come after you." Wise words, but the fear of rocking the corporate boat, of being viewed as "rebellious" or, worse yet, of being labeled the *b*-word, ruled me and I couldn't bring myself to confront anyone. I rationalized that if I fought this fight, students would get hurt in the process, and I didn't want to sacrifice the ministry for the sake of money. What I later realized was that the students would have been fine, and that I allowed some unethical behavior to continue because of my fear of reprisal.

Let me be clear in saying I'm not advocating an obnoxious style of leadership, rather, one that is modeled after Jesus — gracious, strong, and clear in our call. As Christians, we are not to seek after leadership for the glory it will bring us, but for what it will bring to God. By using our God-given abilities of leadership, can we better serve Him, first as Christians, then as women? We have excellent first-century examples to follow:

> We hardly notice, for example, that the first evangelists were women. Those who bore the news of Christ's resurrection were women who took the message, "He's alive!" to a group of men, the disciples, who felt women were not to be believed under these emotional circumstances. If the Word of God is inspired, then this is no accident sneaked into the record by concerned feminists. It explicitly declares that God calls all to deliver His message and that the basis for delivering that message lies in personal commitment, not in the authority structure of either the church or society. . . . In the clamor of this debate in evangelicalism, women must be careful not to sound like the sons of Zebedee talking about their positions in the kingdom. Rather women should engage the debate at the level of service. There is much to be done in extending the kingdom of God. God needs both sexes fully participating in the "call" to change the world.[2]

The barriers we face in youth ministry can be as tangible as the fencing by the Wailing Wall in Jerusalem or as subtle as a whisper of discouragement. These obstacles can be placed there by well-meaning colleagues or erected with our own two hands. In dealing with these barriers, we need to engage a gentle strength combined with godly wisdom so that we don't wound others in seeking to disassemble these hindrances. We need to hold firmly to the attitude portrayed by Christ in the second chapter of Philippians where He broke down barriers with humility and suffering to the point of giving His life. We too, need to understand that we will face suffering when we negotiate barriers. The key will be the attitude with which we do it. We need to acknowledge the pain and anger that sometimes accompanies these barriers, and we need to work with God and close friends to process these emotions and turn them into something productive. For the sake of what God has called us to do and who He has designed us to be, we need to be about the business of breaking down the barriers.

BARRIER BREAKERS

1. What are the barriers you have faced in youth ministry?

2. How have you overcome them?

3. Who has helped you as you've worked to overcome them?

4. How can you help others overcome similar barriers?

Author

Name: *Ginny Olson*

Occupation: *Director of the Youth Ministry Program at North Park College and Director of Youth Ministry Staff Training for the Evangelical Covenant Church.*
Current home: *Algonquin, Illinois*
Marital status: *Looking*
My favorite food is: *Mountain Dew and Twinkies*
The last movie that significantly impacted me was: The United Airlines Safety Video
The style that best reflects me is: *Post-modern*
Favorite childhood memory is: *Killing ants and waving my hand over them to see if I could feel their soul going to heaven*
A good book that I would recommend is: The Autobiography of a Face
If I could do it over: *I'd learn to make meatloaf like my mom's*
If I were a famous painter, I'd paint: *My kitchen; it's gray!*
If I weren't in youth ministry, I'd be: *Sane, happy, and rich*
Words that best describe me: *Dark, cynical, and incurably optimistic*
If I could go anywhere in the world, it would be: *anywhere in Chicago in less than 10 minutes*
My favorite pet is: *Diane's dogs because I don't have to feed them*
The thing that I love about youth ministry is: *All night lock-ins where you sleep on a hard gym floor (Isn't this the reason most people leave youth ministry?)*
One of my passions is to: *Have a clean car someday*
People always think I'm: *Running late . . . and they're right!*
I've learned that: Princess Bride *is the only movie worth watching more than five times, and you should never give junior highers chocolate before a Bible study*
I would like to be remembered for: *Being faithful to what God has called me to do and being who He wants me to be*

EIGHT

You're Not Alone
The benefits of effective networking

by Diane Elliot

Hurricane Gilbert smashed into the island of Jamaica on September 11, 1988, leaving a path of destruction behind. With planes thrown like paper kites, concrete buildings torn in half, and modest homes demolished, the Jamaicans were left without food, electricity, or clean water.

Thousands of miles away, in a suburb of Chicago, a group of high school students from Arlington Countryside Church were devastated by the news. Just two months prior to the disastrous hurricane a small group of students and staff had spent two weeks in Gordontown, a village just outside Kingston, restoring an elementary school and leading a Bible camp. Concerned about their newly-found friends, the students wanted a tangible way to help. With the assistance of the students and staff, I volunteered to administrate the community-wide, six-week project called "Jamaica Relief." The project resulted in collecting 6,000 pounds of food and clothing, as well as donations of $6,000. A team of seven volunteers personally delivered the food, clothing, and funds to Gordontown.

Although the project was a great success, it was not without its difficulties. Midway through the project, I was having a problem finding a way to transport the freight from our suburb of Chicago to West Palm Beach where a mission plane would fly it to Kingston. It seemed that every viable means of transportation that I explored only led to a dead end. When my frustration was at its peak, I called in the reinforcements. I walked into the office of the youth pastor, Dean Bruns, explained the predicament, and asked for advice.

Deep in his own administrative swamp, Dean took the time to listen to the dilemma and make a few phone calls to his carefully developed network. Within minutes, the transportation was secured and I was astounded. What had taken me days of cold-calling, and arguably years off my life, was solved with a few well-chosen phone calls. Now, maybe he was just lucky, but I doubt it. Dean was a master networker and it was then that I realized why. The lesson I learned that day has transformed the way I see networking. My hope had been for Dean to give me some leads that would solve the transportation problem, but what I didn't expect was the long-term impact that networking would have on my ministry, on my life.

I used to categorize networking in the same class as a first date . . . sweaty palms, shaky voice, necessary evil, a means to an end. Although an extrovert, I find it hard to start chit-chatting with someone I don't know. Being a self-proclaimed phone-a-phobic, it's difficult for me to "reach out and touch someone" when that someone is a stranger. Even when I see someone that I think I know in a store, I would rather hide behind a rack of clothes than be forced into awkward conversation while standing at the register. But networking is more than a means to an end. Unlike our secular counterparts that often look at networking as a means for higher profits and better opportunities, we can use the same techniques to better ourselves, enhance our ministry, and build our future, while enriching the lives of those we touch.

SO, WHAT EXACTLY IS NETWORKING?

Here's what some say it is:

> Networking is planting a seed then nurturing it. Some seeds will never grow, but some seeds will."[1]

> "Networking refers to any alliance, relationship or communication with others in your field."[2]

> "Networking is the process of developing and using your contacts for information, advice, and moral support as you pursue your career. It's linking women you know to the women they know in an ever-expanding communications network. It's building a community

of working women, across professional and occupational lines, outside the old boys network. It's helping each other to become more effective in the work world — with more clout, more money, more know-how, more self-confidence. It's beating the system that isolates women as they move up in male-dominated environments. It's asking for help when you need it — knowing *when* you need it, knowing whom and how to ask for it. It's *giving* help, too, serving as a resource for other women. In sum, **it's getting together to get ahead**"[3] (Emphasis added).

Although the latter book was written for businesswomen in 1980, it applies to the similar situations that women in youth ministry find themselves in today. However, there is one major difference between the author's philosophy and a youth minister's philosophy. In youth ministry, our fight is not against gender domination. Rather, our battle is a more significant one. "For our struggle is not against flesh and blood, but against the rulers, against the authorities, against the powers of this dark world and against the spiritual forces of evil in the heavenly realms" (Eph. 6:12). Our battleground is the lives of students, and the enemy is trying every method to sabotage our ministries — including each other, if he can persuade us to do so. In addition, women should not limit their networks to only other women. As coworkers for Christ, we need to network with women *and* men to further the Kingdom.

I believe that networking in ministry is vitally important for your personal well-being and for the well-being of your ministry. Every woman in youth ministry should practice effective networking because it will radically affect three critical areas: first, it will enhance the effectiveness of your current ministries; second, it will help you keep your sanity; and third, it will provide long-term dividends in your future.

NETWORK FOR YOUR MINISTRY

Meeting the Individual Needs of Your Students
Christa March has a ministry to teens that choose to parent their children. Christa's ministry is unique because, in addition to church and para-church agencies, she depends heavily on the

networking services of local social service agencies. Because of this dependence, she has made it a priority to familiarize herself with the available resources, as well as to offer her support when needed. In essence, she has become a clearinghouse for the available resources that are needed for ministering to teen moms in her area. One philosophy that Christa lives by is that she can't possibly know everything, but she can know the people that can give her the answers to the questions that she does have. (For more information, see Teen Mother Choices in Appendix A).

Another ministry that relies heavily on networking for its success is the Home Family Care Network, founded and operated by Felecia Thompson. Located in the heart of Chicago, HFCN shares the love of Christ with the young women and future mothers in their community. It is their philosophy, taken from an ancient African proverb, that it takes an entire village to raise a child. HFCN has a vision to see the people of their community, which has been devastated by sin and decay, brought to a saving knowledge of Christ. They believe it takes an entire community of believers to see that happen.

HFCN utilizes a vast network to staff their diverse programming. Through dedicated volunteers, they have developed need-centered programs that impact the lives of people, thus opening the door for significant relationships with volunteers. This ultimately gives them a platform to share Christ. The programs include: mentoring, single parent workshops, and childbirth classes. The volunteers also demonstrate love tangibly, rather than abstractly, through clothing giveaways and food pantries.

Combining Our Efforts

The northwest suburbs of Chicago has a youth pastors' network that meets together on a monthly basis and organizes one or two events a year, usually one in the fall and one in winter. There are several benefits to doing combined events. First, it eases the administrative and financial burden from one small group. Second, it brings several small groups together to have the excitement and impact of a larger event. Third, it allows students from different youth groups and para-church groups to see other

Christian students from their own area. Many times, the students are surprised to find out that there are so many students from their school that are Christians.

One example of such an event was when the northwest network brought in Pat Hurley to speak. They opened up with a local band followed by a powerful and funny message by Mr. Hurley. Most likely, none of the churches individually could have generated the interest or the resources to pull together the event. But, by pooling their resources, they had a smashing fall kickoff event.

Knowing Community Networks

It is a good idea to keep a notebook of the agencies that you need to know, either in your date book under "referrals" or in a separate notebook. Keep a listing of available resources with their phone numbers and a contact person. It might even be appropriate to contact them before a need arises to familiarize yourself with their services and to request information. Occasionally, they have resources that you can keep on hand to make available to your students. This is a project that could be assigned to a student assistant or a new staff person. That way you would get the information you need as well as familiarizing a new person with available resources in your area.

Following is a suggested list of local resources that are important to incorporate into your network. Some of them you won't necessarily investigate until you need them; others would be good to know now in case there is an immediate need.

   Christian counselors specializing in family and adolescent therapy
   School guidance counselors
   Community police
   Drug rehabilitation center
   Pregnancy counseling center
   Youth service agencies (boys and girls clubs, YMCA, etc.)
   Job placement agencies
   Christian adoption agencies
   Tutors
   Youth workers in your area
   Social service agencies

The bottom line on networking for your ministry is that it better equips you to meet the needs of your students. Whether born from need or from concern for the future, your familiarity with local resources can make a significant contribution to your ministry and ultimately to your students.

NETWORK FOR YOUR SANITY

You are the only one that can take care of you. Simple, but profound. Too often we let the demands of ministry dictate our lives. However, when we allow our schedule to get out of control, our "sanity" often pays the price. To stay in ministry over the long haul, we need to schedule the time to care for ourselves spiritually, physically, mentally, and relationally.

Several years ago, a mutual friend introduced Ginny Olson and me to each other. It was one of those friendships that just worked, a minimal-work-for-maximum-benefits kind of relationship. Before we realized the implications, we had started setting aside time each Monday to get together. We usually met at a restaurant for breakfast or lunch, whatever our schedules allowed. For over three years now, we have met together almost every Monday over a hot cup of coffee and a Diet Coke, talking about ministry, dreams, friendships, and just life. Over time, one of our dreams became a reality as we founded and developed Journey Publications, Inc., a ministry encouraging the leadership development of volunteer and professional women in youth ministry.

We felt Journey was important because we realized the significance of having friends in ministry with whom we could share our joys and burdens. Many times, as youth workers, we are isolated from others that share the same passion for youth. Making matters worse, as women in ministry, we are often surrounded by male youth workers who don't quite know how to fit us into their network. More than ever, we need to draw some significant individuals into our lives that can encourage us toward wholeness, not isolation. People who will open the doors that need opening. People that will walk with us on our exciting journey in youth ministry.

Networking for Support

After being a volunteer in a high school youth ministry for a few years, I realized the importance of support from other youth workers outside my ministry. I was very involved with the students and staff but had little to do with other youth ministers outside of our ministry. At a network youth event, quite by accident, I ran into a woman that was a youth worker from the local para-church organization. There was no immediate chemistry that initiated our friendship. Rather, for me it was curiosity about how she was managing to survive the daily rigors of youth ministry. We had lunch together and I found that, by listening to her ministry stories, I was encouraged. It was tremendous to know there was someone out there who understood the excitement as well as the perils of youth ministry. Networking for support is the glue that holds us together when the external forces of ministry try to tear us apart.

My husband Dave is a residential home builder. One of the things that he has done to better himself and increase his wisdom when faced with difficult decisions is to develop a group of men that he calls his "Wise Guys." These carefully selected men are not necessarily aware of their status or of the others that hold the position with them. The "Wise Guys" are men of various vocations, ages, and geographic locations that have shown a personal interest in Dave. After developing a trusting relationship of mutual respect with each individual, Dave has earned the right to ask for, and occasionally give, advice. In the face of a decision, he contacts the individuals and bounces ideas off them for feedback. After receiving enough information to make a wise decision with confidence, he makes his choices and moves ahead.

Another benefit of the "Wise Guys" is that they offer more than business advice. Most of the men are dedicated followers of Christ who seek to honor God through their businesses. Thus, their words of wisdom often reflect their concern for Dave personally and spiritually, as well as professionally.

In youth ministry we also need our circle of wise women and men who can support and encourage our work. In fact, it is even more important that we have support in ministry than in secular business. In ministry we are in the business of permanently changing hearts, not making a temporary profit. Our adversary wants nothing more than to sabotage our efforts and ruin our reputation. We need to have concerned individuals surrounding us to offer advice, encouragement, and prayer for our ministry and for us personally.

Networking for Sharpening

After being out of school for over eight years, I decided to go back and finish my bachelor's degree. I had audited several youth ministry classes at Trinity Evangelical Divinity School, but I had put off finishing my degree because my time was limited, and I was over two years away from completion. As the doors opened for me to concentrate on finishing my B.A., I cleared my schedule and put all my efforts toward my studies. I anticipated the long classes and mounds of homework. What I didn't anticipate was the tremendous mental stimulation that I had lacked for a long time. After I got into the study routine and the cobwebs were cleared from my dusty brain, I actually enjoyed the challenges. Each course was filled with a new adventure. Even geology was a wonder that I had never dared tackle before. Theology was especially challenging since I had grown up in a Christian home and not often questioned my theological views.

One of my professors (who never gave me better than a B, no matter how hard I tried) was determined to challenge me to think beyond my self-imposed constraints. At first, it was very uncomfortable because I thought that challenging my beliefs would somehow weaken them. The opposite was true, however. With a deeper knowledge of the Word, I could put my passion behind the things that I found to be truth and loosen my grip on the things that had been traditional rather than biblical.

Each of us needs the mental sharpening that education can bring. However, it doesn't necessarily need to come in the form of school. Oftentimes, it can come through friendships with mentally stimulating people. The goal, however, is not to pick only people that are like yourself. We tend to coccoon with people of like kind. Although more challenging to relate to, individuals with different views help us to think in new ways. It is a rare gift when you can find unique individuals with whom you can maintain good friendships while agreeing to disagree on certain topics.

Networking for Accountability

We all have different types of friendships that meet different needs in our lives: acquaintances, "Wise Guys," and mentally stimulating individuals. But, more than anything, we all need trusted and valued friends who are willing to keep us accountable. These friends are the ones who know us inside and out. These are the ones we go to when life gets difficult and we need a shoulder to cry on. These are the ones who allow us to be *real,* without fearing rejection. These are the few who will stand by us in spite of our spiritual doubts, impure thoughts, or deep secrets. They are the friends who know us on stage and off and are willing to give honest feedback, even when it hurts. These friends are the ones who go the distance through time and difficult moments.

I once had a time when I was struggling with some inappropriate feelings that were trying to tear me apart. The first step for me to deal appropriately with these feelings was to express them to a trusted friend. It was through her insight and helpful evaluation that I was able to get them under control. Without the honest sharing during that emotionally difficult time, I might have been overwhelmed by those feelings and acted on them inappropriately. In essence, she saved me from myself. Sometimes we need friends like that to keep us on the right path.

NETWORK FOR YOUR FUTURE

I was the transportation coordinator for a leadership conference in Estes Park, Colorado one spring. During the conference, one of the attendees needed to be driven to the Denver airport, a round trip of four hours. I tried to get one of my volunteers to make the trip, but all of their schedules were consumed with other tasks. Because I was the one in charge, and the attendee needed to get to Denver, I had to take him . . . but I didn't have to be happy about it.

I had heard the attendee's name, Brian McClairen, before, but I had never met him. Our first meeting was a flurry of throwing bags in the car, giving instructions to the volunteer staying behind, and Brian saying good-bye to his wife. As with any first meeting, I wasn't thrilled with the idea of being alone with someone I didn't know for two hours. Over the years I had mastered the art of chit-chat when necessary; however, the critical element lies in the willingness of the other participant to return the verbal volleys. Not knowing Brian, I was worried that he might not want to return the volleys. Fortunately, Brian was a master of the sport, and it wasn't long until we found out that we had many friends and acquaintances in common. Exploring further, I found that he was a pastor of a new and growing church in the Washington, D.C. area. Better yet, he was looking for a youth leader for his church and asked if I knew anyone who might be interested. I immediately came up with two women who were in the process of exploring their future options for youth ministry. I gave Brian the names, and he contacted them the next day.

Months prior to my trip to Colorado, Saundra Hensel had expressed to me the desire to make a ministry move. The position that she was in was not fully using her gifts and abilities, and she was ready for a change. Knowing that information, other youth ministry friends and I kept an ear open to any ministry positions that Saundra might be interested in. Eventually, it paid off. Brian contacted Saundra and a few weeks later, the church flew her out to D.C. for an interview. One month later I drove with Saundra from the Midwest to the East Coast, where she is now the Director of Student Ministries at Cedar Ridge Community Church. That's networking for your future.

Knowing the Players in the Field
In youth ministry it's good to know about other ministries out there and what they are doing to reach kids. Not only is this beneficial for your current ministry, but it also allows you to have future career dreams. One way to keep up with other ministries is to receive a youth ministry publication like *Youth Worker Journal,* published by Youth Specialties or *GROUP* magazine, published by Group Publishing. These publications have a variety of contributors, writing on relevant topics concerning youth ministry. Another way that opens the door for face-to-face training and interaction is to attend a youth ministry conference like **The Incredible Journey,** for women in youth ministry, or gen-

eral training for youth workers like **Youth Specialties, Kidstitute** (sponsored by Group Publishing), **National Network of Youth Ministries,** or any of the other seminars listed in Appendix A. Conferences give practical training as well as help individuals to develop a broader vision of their ministry and the resources available to them. The other benefit is that such conferences can be an encouraging atmosphere where you can be affirmed and stretched.

For me, conferences have been a place where I have been ministered to, refreshed my passion for students, and met individuals who have significantly impacted my life. It is not always the speakers that make the biggest impression, however. Sometimes it's the person I sit next to in a seminar, or the person that I am introduced to by a mutual friend. Many of the people that I have stumbled on at youth ministry events over the years, I still keep in contact with, and they have become faithful colleagues and friends.

Knowing Where You Want to Go

When I started in youth ministry, I had no idea I would be in ministry for many years. I thought I would volunteer for a year or two, then get back to whatever it was I was doing before I started youth ministry. At the very most, I thought I might stay in ministry until I was thirty-five and then "get on with my life." I thought that after thirty-five I would be too old to have any significant relationships with students. *I couldn't have been more wrong!*

There is no magical numerical age that dictates when one should exit ministry. God has a way of taking a willing heart, at any age and using it to impact students' lives. Contrary to past tradition, being in youth ministry is not as narrowly defined as being a young, male youth pastor at a church. It's so much more than that. Being in youth ministry can take many shapes, molding to your specific personality and availability. A youth worker can be a woman who gives one hour a week to spend time with a student in discipleship. It can be having students over once a month to bake cookies and play together with your young children. It can be spending one, two, or three weeks a year at a youth summer camp or leading a short-term mission project to a foreign country. Whatever avenues God allows you to utilize to reach students, that's youth ministry. We need to think in terms of lifelong youth ministry, not just one year or two of madness followed by a step into oblivion. Kids don't need short-term fun and activity at the expense of long-term, steady relationships.

With these things in mind, youth workers have the opportunity to explore the future with openness and excitement. If you are interested in being a full-time church or para-church youth worker, pursue that avenue with all your heart. **Inter-Christo, Youth Specialties,** and **Journey Publications** all have youth ministry job listings. If, however, you are a trained professional in another vocation and can give only a porition of your time to youth ministry, that's great too. Contact your local church or para-church organization and let them know what time and gifts you have to offer. Or, if you're a woman who started out in full-time youth ministry, married, and started a family and can't or don't want to continue in full-time ministry, don't lose hope. Just change your ministry methods to fit your lifestyle. A volunteer can be a lifesaver to a full-time worker needing some adults for one-on-one student discipleship. Or, if you don't have the time, or there's isn't an official program available for volunteering, take on one student, a neighbor, a friend's teenager, or a nephew or niece, as your personal project. Spend quality time with him or her. Do things together. Spend time talking about how you see God working in your life. Be a living testimony to that one special person. God can use your availability and bless it abundantly. The key is to actively pursue whatever means you have to minister to students.

Knowing What It Takes to Get Where You Want to Go
Once you have determined where you want to go in the future (see chapter 6 for more information on this topic), part of the fun is mapping out a plan to achieve your goals. There is a school of thought that says it is anti-Christian to have ministry goals. For some reason, goals are equated with not trusting God for the future. My hunch is that, when Christ came to earth, He had a pretty clear goal in mind. By being fervent in our prayers and seeking wise advice, we can move forward with confidence, knowing that God desires our ministries to be effective. By using

our best resources, best planning, and best efforts we can do our part to build God's kingdom. Questions to ask yourself include:

- How has God wired me?
- What are the assets that I have available to me? Time, talents, treasures?
- How can I serve God most effectively?
- Do my "Wise Guys" concur with my ideas?
- Where would I like to be in three years? Ten Years?
- What do I need to do to get there? Immediately? Next year? In five years?

By creatively exploring where you want to be, and how you can get there, you can be a more effective minister in the lives of students.

CONCLUSION:

Networking is a lifeline for people in ministry. We were never *meant* to serve alone. Although sometimes it is difficult and takes intentional effort, by networking you can enhance your ministry, keep your emotional sanity, explore your future, and, in the process, become the person God wants you to be.

BARRIER BREAKERS

1. What networks do you already have in place in your life and ministry?

2. What networks do you need to develop to help bring balance to your personal life? Ministry?

3. What are your future goals that networking can help you achieve?

4. What are some of the steps you need to take to help you achieve these goals?

Author

Name: *Diane Elliot*

Occupation: *Wife, author, speaker, youth worker, Journey president . . . basically an entrepreneur*
Current home: *Long Grove, Illinois*
Marital status: *Yes, for nearly half of my life*
Kids: *My two dogs, Stormy (11) and Pepper (9)*
My favorite food is: *Chocolate*
The last movie that significantly impacted me was: Forrest Gump

The style that best reflects me is: *Eclectic*

Favorite childhood memory: *Being at our family cabin in Northern Wisconsin*

A good book that I would recommend is: The Upside of Down *by Joseph Stowell*

Nobody believes: *I have been married for 15 years (I was a child bride!)*

If I could do it over: *I would have dropped the expectations a long time ago*

I'd give anything to meet: *Whoopie Goldberg*

If I could change one thing about myself: *I'd speed up my metabolism by 100 rpm's*

If I weren't in youth ministry, I'd be: *The owner and CEO of several companies*

Words that best describe me are: *Spontaneous, dreamer, visionary*

In my lifetime I still want to: *Travel the world and write a screen play*

It really bugs me when: *I'm not in control*

One of my passions is to: *Expose students to missions*

People always think I'm: *Organized (Fooled them!)*

If there is one thing that I would like to tell my colleagues, it would be: *In the words of Winston Churchill, "Never, never, never give up."*

In my life I've learned that: *"It's the* hard *that makes it good." (Thanks Tom Hanks! From the movie* A League of Their Own.*)*

NINE

What Men Can Do to Help
One man's journey toward awareness

by Tim McLaughlin

Before I knew enough to ogle a twentysomething female, I had one for my junior high youth leader. She had a blonde coworker, but it was the duskier Elaine I remember. She smiled a lot during our Sunday evening youth meetings in the brick-and-concrete basement of my Baptist church. She took twenty or so of us barely pubescent kids on a nighttime yachting excursion on the Columbia River one August. I remember it was August, because, when I got home late, my mother was frightened: North Vietnam, she told me, had attacked a pair of our ships in the Gulf of Tonkin.

When I was in high school — which is to say, when my youth leader was an up-and-coming male seminarian who loved talking sports, hot cars, and the need for personal Bible study — my former youth leader Elaine married a gentle giant of a man and departed for the mission field somewhere in Central America. British Honduras, maybe. I lost track of Elaine about the same time I figured out that British Honduras had become Belize.

Thirty years later on Santa Catalina Island, I was lounging in a spartan dining hall that had just disgorged itself of 100 rowdy high school campers. A few counselors, I among them, were chatting absently in the abrupt quietness. As the conversation evolved, I realized I was among a small but vigorous group of ordained female youth pastors who questioned me pointedly, though politely, about the dearth of women in the speaker lineups at youth ministry events — and, in particular, in the pages of a youth ministry magazine I edit. Why was there typically only one female writer in a male-dominated table of contents? Didn't

I understand that I only compounded the difficulty these youth ministers had in convincing their female students that youth ministry — or any ministry — is a valid, open, and rewarding career for women?

These two memories of female youth pastors — one from my early adolescence, the other from only a few years ago — tell me something about the effect pastoral women have had on me. The pair of memories are curious to me, maybe because I never thought twice about a woman being my junior high youth pastor. (Maybe the deacons in that Baptist church thought twice about it. I wouldn't know.) The innocence of a rapidly evaporating childhood, maybe. Whatever it was, it was gone by the time I was on the hot seat in Catalina, when I tried not to be defensive. Really. But through these female pastors' experiences I saw, for a moment at least, what male-dominated ministry represented to them.

From such conversations with ministering women, I am only beginning to learn how to demonstrate and confirm with my attitudes and words their irreplaceable value in ministry. Here are a few habits and insights I've tried to cultivate.

STEP OUTSIDE OF YOUR COMFORT ZONE

Every now and again it's good to take a look from the outside. Outside your own perspective, your own denominational persuasion or practice, or even your own gender. Rent *Tootsie*. Read *Women's Reality*. Tell your female associate if she'll read your copy of *Iron John*, you'll read *Women Who Run with the Wolves*.

Four of us counselors started an easy conversation (at yet another youth retreat) about a denomination's opinion about a particular conference. It quickly advanced into an intense, face-to-face debate between two among us: a pair of associate pastors, one female, the other male. The argument that Saturday afternoon spread itself over theology, Bible interpretation, church upbringings, sexism, imagination, the wisdom of overshooting the mark in order to compensate for a long-standing deficiency, and more. She was trying to verbalize that, despite the charges of heresy directed at the conference by some, the notion behind it touched off in her deep, visceral feelings of being left out, of being set aside, passed over. Get over the radical language of the event, she said in so many words, and get in touch with what this meant for women in the Christian church — at least with what it meant for me.

"But how can you ignore language if we're to evaluate truth and error by language?" he asked. As much as he sympathized with her sentiment and collective backlog of exclusion, he just couldn't bring himself to jettison the black-and-white verbal from the imaginative essence.

Next morning, a Sunday, the celebration of the Lord's Supper gave communion a whole new meaning for me. There they were up front, my two ordained friends, officiating in casual camp vestments. Yesterday they were nose to nose in frustrated, argumentative discourse. Now they were side by side — literally, spiritually, relationally — and agents of the peace of God to all of us in the campground's chapel. As this woman and man served us the body and blood of Christ, I knew they brought to this sacrament the broadening influence of yesterday's conversation, whose ideas still percolated, still simmered in them as they tried to understand each other's spiritual experience and theological perceptions.

TRY TALKING DIFFERENTLY

I asked my wife, her church's youth director, if she had noticed my noble attempts at inclusive language lately. Her silence irked me. So I felled the silence. "You know," I reminded her (I have to remind her? It isn't obvious?), "I've been deliberately saying stuff like 'his or her' instead of 'his.'"

She pondered it a moment longer and said it's one of those things she doesn't notice readily. "But," she added, "I'd notice if you didn't speak inclusively."

It goes further than semantics. One of the most insulting moments in a friend's experience occurred when the president of the seminary she was attending (she was one of very, very few women enrolled) called her in and asked if she'd like to be his secretary. She thought, *I'm a seminarian, preparing for full-time ministry, pursuing an advanced degree, and he asks me if I want to be his* secretary? *Does he call in male students and ask them if they want to be his secretary?*

"No thanks," she said. "I'm not trained to be a secretary — and besides, I want to graduate early, so I don't have time."

Such insensitivity wasn't limited to the administration, she remembers. Fellow seminarians opened conversations with "Are you part-time?" or "Is your husband a student?" Granted, she was something of an oddity, at that seminary at least. I would probably be as tempted as the next man to lapse into old mental and verbal habits. But the habits must go if we really believe what we say about partnership in ministry and in life.

Your new habits of thinking about and speaking to women may be immensely meaningful to your female colleagues. Then again, they may be more amused than affirmed. Which brings us to this observation.

DON'T ASSUME ANYTHING

Understand that your associate may or may not care about, detect, or have been wounded by sexism. Don't assume that because yours is a mainline church, the female pastor on staff with you is a feminist; she may be staunchly conservative. (Herein lies a Catch-22 for female youth pastors of evangelical persuasion: the very churches inclined to hire female pastors — mainline churches — cool off when they discover that their female candidates are conservative. Yet the churches in which such women feel doctrinally at home — evangelical churches — tend not to hire women to fill their pastoral positions due, supposedly and ironically, to doctrinal reasons.)

Neither should you assume that your new female associate entered the profession in reaction to unmitigated male hegemony in the church for two millennia. There are female youth ministers who spent their own youth group days with only female leaders. They can't imagine what it's like to have a man as a youth leader. When they think "youth worker," they see a "she" — not a "he."

Just don't jump to conclusions about the women you work with professionally. Having grown up in a church with as many female as male leaders, Lynette spent only a couple years on the staff of a male-led church before she became disenchanted with male pastoral attitude. Andrea, on the other hand, was unchurched until a young adult. She then began working with a heavily male church staff. And to this day, she has had only positive experiences and enjoys working with a staff that is, as far as gender and leadership goes, very traditional. Some things you just can't predict. Talk with women, don't assume anything.

REMEMBER THE SIMPLE THINGS

Etiquette, respect, dignity, and equal treatment—that is, treat your ministry associates as professional pastors first, and as Republicans, Floridians, or women a distant second. This will go a long way toward resolving gender issues, without ever bringing up the gender issue per se.

A word about respect as it pertains to youth ministry. The humor of male youth ministers tends to pick up on eccentricities that individuals don't have much control over—human or physical frailties, for example. The humor of female youth ministers, on the other hand, tends to take on those in power—like the greeting-card gag that depicts a '50s-era mother and daughter. The daughter asks, "Mommy, why do women tend to live longer than men?"

"I don't know, honey," the mother responds, "but we think it's a pretty good system."

So if you're male and are given to spicing up your youth talks with crass comments you find funny, rethink your humor and what it may be communicating to your kids about dignity and personal worth. Humor shouldn't be at the expense of others.

DESEXUALIZE YOUR RELATIONSHIPS WITH YOUR FEMALE COLLEAGUES

Know your buttons, know when they're pushed, and know how you intend to react when they're pushed. It's probably fruitless trying to avoid getting them pushed, so don't waste time feeling guilty when they are. Acknowledge it, remind yourself what it is you want out of life and your relationships, and get on with it. If you cannot desexualize (in this sense) your relationships with female staff members, then you'll spend your life compensating for pushed buttons by reigning yourself in. And that's OK too.

Author and sociologist Andrew M. Greeley leaves no doubt about the light years between temptation and sin:

> What matters about temptation is not how long it lasts, not how seductive it is, but whether we finally give in to it either by actually doing what the temptation invites us to do or by making up our mind that we would if we could do so. The length, the attractiveness, the frequency, the intensity of the temptation do not move the temptation one inch toward sin.[1]

At least in the current climate, you won't be pitied, teased, or ostracized for resisting another's advances (or for denying your own). Take heart — a kind of chic sexual squeamishness is fashionable these days. In fact, our unchurched culture has outstripped evangelical Christians right and left: a dinner party with plenty of mineral water and nonalcoholic drinks is socially appropriate. At least in the trendier sections of California, to be seen smoking is as boorish as not smoking was twenty years ago. High school sex education classes are now pushing abstinence as good public policy, thanks to HIV/AIDS and many millions of taxpayers' dollars for abortions or obstetric and pediatric care, for the nearly inevitable AFDC that waits for unwed teen mothers.

It's not just Christians anymore who are fleeing from the appearance of workplace evil at the water cooler. What I remember of my own youth pastor's denunciation of our teenage necking pales beside today's vitriolic condemning of office flirtation and its implied sexism. The prohibitive vigor of which is, curiously, downright Puritan; although the motive is less obedience to God's Word than it is "Love long, don't invade others' space with your habits, and if you must have your little sexual indiscretions, the least you can do is to show a little courtesy and tact toward the one with whom you're planning to be indiscreet. And whatever you do, don't let your indiscretion incur public cost."

And then there are the legal perils of women and men working together — not just at secular worksites, but in church offices and Sunday School rooms and at ministry conventions. The "appearance of evil" is now an "allegation of sexual harassment." Litigiously, even at church — especially at church — you've got to cover yourself. Church policies about side hugs only, open doors when counseling the opposite sex, and limits on working late hours with each other may protect you legally.

On the other hand, unless you know what you want and what you don't want — from professional relationships, from client relationships, from your marriage — no amount of behavioral guidelines will protect you spiritually (though they will protect you legally).

All this to say, of course you can't take appearances lightly. Only realize that the limits you impose to legally protect yourself and your church do not necessarily protect your spirit, your mind, and your emotions.

Several years ago I went forward in my small church to take communion. At the front stood not only the church's pastor, but also a married couple. She held the loaf; he, the cup. When the line moved me to her, it was her words, her voice — "The body of Christ, broken for you, Tim" — that undid me. It was the sacramental ministry to me through my friend that awoke in me for the first time the taste of what women must feel who are trying on the truth the Apostle Paul wrote of: a church in which there is neither black nor WASP, blue collar nor management, male nor female — for we are all one in Christ Jesus.

BARRIER BREAKERS

1. **What are your assumptions about female youth workers? Male youth workers?**

2. Why is it important for youth workers to use inclusive language?

3. What books would help you understand someone else's perspective on this topic?

4. Who are you meeting with to discuss becoming more aware of the other gender's perspective?

Author

Name: *Tim McLaughlin*

Occupation: *Editor, Youth Specialties*
Birthplace: *Whittier, California*
Current home: *Santee, California (suburban San Diego)*
Marital status: *Married*
Children: *Four (bookend girls 19 & 7, boys 15 & 17)*
The last movie that significantly impacted me was: The Remains of The Day *(The Mask impacted me, but not significantly—though it made me laugh hysterically!)*
The style that best reflects me is: *Oregon outback*
A good book that I would recommend is: A Prayer for Owen Meany
I've never been able to: *Decently downhill ski*
I'd give anything to meet: *Garrison Keillor. But then, I've met him once already, and didn't know what to say. Sheesh.*
If I weren't in youth ministry, I'd be: *An outdoor educator*
Words that best describe me: *Thought you'd get me to reveal my innate and well-concealed but vast ego, huh? No deal!*
I love to: *Fly in an F-anything and have lots of local grandchildren (but not quite yet)*
If I could go anywhere in the world, it would be: *Ireland*
It really bugs me when: *I just hate seeing myself in my kids*
One of my passions is to: *Read aloud*
People always think I'm: *A pleasant fellow (Hah! Fools!)*
I've learned that: *I am not nearly as pleasant as I seem*
I would like to be remembered for: *Loved God. Loved kids.*

TEN

Men Influencing Female Students

Healthy relationships with young women

by Jim Burns

Healthy, positive youth work is most often based on positive, healthy role models. Not to oversimplify, but almost all long-lasting results in youth ministry are based not so much on programs as on relationships.

Why it has taken some churches so long to figure out that students need healthy, positive role models from both genders is a mystery. Unfortunately, until recent years, youth ministry was mainly a "male thing." (All one has to do is look at the list of speakers for a major youth event.) Without providing both female and male leadership, we've done a disservice to the church and our students. I want young women to walk away from youth group with the thought, "I want to be like Laurie," not, "I want to marry a youth leader like Jim." Same sex role models are absolutely essential for good youth ministry and good role modeling of the Christian life. At the same time, because so much youth work is modeling, we also need healthy opposite sex role models. In today's world, where can a young woman or young man build a relationship with someone of the opposite sex in a safe, secure, healthy, Christ-centered atmosphere? Frankly, it's getting more difficult to find a place to build this kind of a relationship.

OPPOSITE SEX ROLE MODELS

As a male youth worker and a father of three girls (I'm out numbered four to one in our home!), I constantly see the incredible need for a healthy male relationship in the lives of young women. Cathy and I participate in a weekly married couples group at our church. Every one of the women in our group say they had no positive Christian male role models when they were students. Today, so many kids are being raised with "absent fathers." Obviously, it is crucial for the church to provide a healthy male influence.

During our twenty plus years of youth ministry and marriage, springtime has meant, among other things, time for the youth group "sex talks." I don't know why we always use spring to talk in the group about the *S* word, but we do. Generally, we split up the group. The first week Cathy takes the girls and I deal with the guys. The next week is what the kids look forward to most and, frankly, it often generates a more lively discussion. That's when Cathy takes the guys and I have the girls in my group. We basically tell them the same information, but from an opposite sex perspective. When it comes time for questions and discussion, the girls pound me with questions about what a guy thinks, and the guys urge Cathy to fill them in on what girls are thinking.

I hope you are creating similar opportunities for safe cross-gender feedback. When students have stable, nurturing adults of the opposite sex with whom they can build relationships, you are well on your way to an effective youth ministry. We so often place such a high priority on programming and events, when, in reality, one of the main purposes of an event is to nurture safe relationships that will model and witness the love of God.

Right in the midst of this chapter, let's try an experiment. Take thirty seconds to write down on a piece of paper the five most influential sermons in your life. Now take thirty seconds to write down the five people who have influenced your life the most.

If you are like most of us, you can't name five sermons from your entire lifetime but you find it much easier to think of influential people in your life. Who were these people? You probably didn't jot down the names of famous people. Your list is likely full of plain-old, regular people like you and me. Perhaps you came up with a list that included a parent, teacher, coach, pastor, or even a youth worker. One of our most important jobs in youth ministry is to develop more than surface relationships with the guys and girls God has entrusted to us in our group.

THE FATHER IMAGE

Every leader in our youth group loved Karen. She was an eleventh grader who came to every event we sponsored and, on a regular basis, she told us how wonderful the youth group was and how wonderful we were as her leaders. We nicknamed her "the clinger" because she was always clinging onto the arm of one of the male leaders. Often this cute young girl would run up to me and enthusiastically hug me. One day in a staff meeting, one of the male volunteers shared with the rest of us that he felt uncomfortable with all the physical attention he was getting from Karen. Some of the women on staff chimed in that they thought her display of affirmation and affection with men was almost inappropriate. Then they all looked at me, their fearless youth pastor, for the answer. Finally, one of the volunteers said, "Jim, I think you should talk to Karen." Nobody bailed me out, so I said OK.

At youth group that night Karen came running up to me as she always did and offered a bear hug. I watched her during our meeting, and she basically moved from male leader to male leader offering shoulder rubs and lots of touching. That evening I asked Karen if we could talk for a moment. After an uncomfortable silence I began. "Karen, I hope you know how much we all love and appreciate you and that you are very special to this group. I want to bring up a sensitive issue. It's come to my attention that although I don't think you mean anything wrong by it, you are possibly offering too much display of physical affection with our male leaders."

Tears welled up in her eyes and she immediately got defensive with all the statements you would think she would say. I let her talk. Then she started to cry. She blurted out, "My father left me when I was eight. The last words he said to me were 'I'm moving to Las Vegas and I'll call you this weekend and we'll plan when we can get together.' He ended with the words 'I love you.'" With tears in her eyes she cried, "But he didn't love me because he didn't call back for two years and then only to tell me and Mom he was gonna get remarried."

I realized right then that here was a young woman who desperately needed a positive father image. Like so many other dads, her father wasn't there for Karen, providing the loving, strong arms. Her clinging was not so much a sexual flirtation as an honest need to relate to a male role model.

In conversations we had after that evening, Karen revealed another side of her that none of us at the church had really seen. She was a victim of sexual abuse. It was almost always the same story. She would display physical affection to an older man, and he would then seduce her into a sexual relationship. She wasn't looking for sex. She was searching desperately for the relationship she craved from her own biological father.

SETTING RELATIONAL BOUNDARIES

When we look at Karen's story in light of the Gospel, the problem becomes, how do we introduce a very foreign concept to her — the unconditional love of "Abba"? The "Karens" of our world will seldom accept the simple, beautiful message of Jesus' sacrificial death, because they have mainly experienced just the opposite from men. Our job is, yes, to give girls like Karen the Gospel but not in a relational vacuum, rather in the context of relationships and modeling. Paul challenged Timothy to not only give out the Gospel of God but to give our people our very lives as well. Relational and incarnational ministry is what will change lives.

Given the reality of the importance of relationships, how can we, who are male, minister to the girls in our group in a safe, healthy environment? Unfortunately, for many, the pendulum has swung from spending a great deal of time in opposite sex relationships to many men and women being fearful of sexual abuse allegations. Both extremes are unhealthy for the kids.

Some of the most wonderful ministry relationships I've ever had have been with young women for whom I was able to care within the context of proper boundaries. Cheryl is one of those women I got to know while she was a junior high student, and we have remained close through the years. She is now a youth worker and married to a pastor. Her father was never close to his girls, and he divorced the family when she was in junior high. Cheryl and I built a healthy relationship around the church. She came in and volunteered to help with whatever chores I gave her. My wife Cathy invited her home for dinner on a regular basis. We felt it was important for her to view and experience a healthy marriage and a Christian home. To my knowledge, I was never alone with her in a compromising setting (more about that in a moment) and there was never inappropriate touch. I found that by including her in my life and my family's life, we could develop a close relationship without the possible negative male/female barriers.

The big word here is boundaries. If you set standards and boundaries before you ever get involved in ministry relationships, you will have a much more effective ministry. Listed below are my own set of boundaries for ministry with the opposite sex.

1. Never meet with a girl or woman in a secluded setting.
This means I choose not even to share a meal or a Coke alone. This also includes driving and being in their home without their parents present. For an older guy like me, I choose to not be in the home alone with their mothers also.

2. Same sex discipleship and one-on-one relationships are most effective.
Although discipleship can be done in a variety of ways, I do believe it is safer and more effective to have deeper ministry relationships with the same sex. If the girls or guys need the opposite sex perspective, then set up time when you all can get together.

3. A diversity of staff is a must.
Because the best youth ministry is relational, it seems only normal that different kids will relate to different youth workers. A holistic approach to role modeling is to provide the students with "mother" and "father" figures as well as older "brother" and "sister" relationships. I even know a great youth group in California who uses "grandparents" to fulfill an important missing ingredient in the lives of their students.

4. Staff members should not date students in the youth group.
I was eighteen and a freshman in college. She was seventeen and Miss Arcadia, California. She wanted to date me and, in fact, she invited me to her homecoming event. In the worst way I

wanted to go. Actually, I almost gave up my youth ministry position to date her. However, a very wise person told me that if I dated a student in the group, I was setting my ministry up for failure. He was right.

5. Confront any leader with even the slightest danger sign.
Far too many leaders use the youth group to meet their own personal needs. We had to ask a very dynamic young man to quit our youth staff. He hadn't dated much, if any, in high school or college and now he was enjoying all the attention of the ninth grade girls just a little too much. He knew our boundaries and the moment I heard that he and one of the girls talked out in front of her house in his car alone for three hours until past midnight, I asked him to take a sabbatical from leadership in the group. He vehemently denied that anything questionable happened and said that they had just been talking. I believed him, but the point was still that he knew the boundaries and he went past them. As a youth pastor, part of my role is protection and prevention.

6. No sexual innuendoes or flirting should be tolerated between youth and staff.
Let's face it, sometimes the talk gets just a little out of hand. I'm not asking everyone to be a prude. I do believe, however, that we are called by biblical standards to remain free of behavior which could be construed as sexual.

After reading these six simple statements, some may be thinking *what an old-fashioned, almost legalistic, approach to opposite sex relationships with youth. After all, isn't it the 90s?* That's exactly why I've set high standards and boundaries: it is the 90s and one slip can cost you an otherwise excellent ministry. Is it more difficult to minister in the confines of these boundaries? Yes, I believe it is a more difficult task. For me, however, the possible negative experiences of not having these boundaries far outweigh the positive. Males can and must build relationships with young women, yet in the context of healthy role models.

It's very exciting to see a new wave of youth ministry happening in our world, with much more emphasis on positive role models. It's extremely encouraging to see women taking an active role in youth ministry leadership. Just the advent of books like this tells us that God is doing a great new work in youth ministry. I, for one, applaud the incredibly important role women are playing in youth ministry leadership and the sensitivity men are developing to cross-gender ministry.

BARRIER BREAKERS

1. What are some additional benefits to having cross-gender role models?

2. How can you increasingly support cross-gender modeling in your ministry?

3. What cross-gender boundaries do you have in place in your ministry?

4. How can you facilitate discussion of gender issues in your youth ministry?

Author

Name: *Jim Burns*

Occupation: *President, National Institute of Youth Ministry*
Birthplace: *Orange, California*
Current home: *Dana Point, California*
Marital status: *20 years to Cathy*
Children: *Christy (11), Rebecca (9), Heidi (7)*
My favorite food is: *Pasta*
The last movie that significantly impacted me *was*: The Lion King

The style that best reflects me is: *Casual*
Favorite childhood memory: *Little League*
A good book that I would recommend is: Connecting *by Bobby Clinton*
Nobody knows I'm: *Someone who cries at movies*
If I could do it over: *I'd take more vacations*
I'd give anything to meet: *Billy Graham*
If I were a famous painter, I'd paint: *Ocean scenes*
If I could change one thing about myself: *I'd be more physically disciplined*
If I weren't in youth ministry, I'd be: *Playing sports*
If I could live anywhere in the world, it would be: *Maui, Hawaii*
My favorite place to spend time with God is: *Maui, on a beach*
One of my passions is to: *Speak to kids*
The thing that I love most about youth ministry is: *Making a difference*

ELEVEN

Thinking Creatively

Programming ideas for women ministering to girls

by Karen Grant

Being a young woman in today's world is, in itself, a challenge. However, being a young *Christian* woman in today's morally deteriorating world is seemingly impossible. In junior high and high school there are many pressures and situations that challenge the maturing faith of students. The support of a local church and youth ministry can provide young men and women with friendships, wholesome activities and programs, biblical teaching, and an atmosphere for spiritual growth. Is there a place for "girls only" oriented programs, activities, and ministries within a youth group or parachurch organization? If so, what are the benefits to the individual girls, staff, and ministry as a whole?

In answer to the first question, most youth workers believe there is a place for "girls only" programs. Most youth experiences, such as education and activities, are coeducational. Even the majority of church activities are planned for guys and girls, leaving little time for girls to experience individual attention for developing healthy female friendships, discipling relationships, and mentoring. However, with some specialized programming to promote gender-based activities, youth groups can foster these relationships.

It is much easier for programs for girls to be implemented if one or more staff women (paid or volunteer) take the initiative for organizing or facilitating the creation of programs. Even though male youth staff may understand and believe in the need and benefits of programming for girls, programs probably will be better received by the girls in the ministry if planned by staff women. One benefit then becomes girls seeing staff women as leaders with skills and talents of their own.

Many programs can involve the girls themselves assisting with the planning and implementation of programs. Girls can develop their leadership skills, find what their gifts and talents are, and learn to work as a member of a team.

As staff women work with girls to organize activities, relationships develop and leadership training and development take place. Staff women also develop relationships with each other when working together on special programs. Mentoring relationships between staff women can also begin to develop through working together for girls in their ministry.

Benefits of "girls only" programs to the entire ministry include the increase and deepening of same sex relationships. It is important for young men and women to learn how to develop same sex friendships before developing opposite sex relationships. It is also important for them to maintain those same gender friendships through the dating years and beyond. Having same gender programs and discipling groups can foster these friendships.

Programming for girls is more likely to occur, with all the positive benefits, with the support of the youth leadership. Girls only programs must enhance and not compete with the programs and goals of the youth ministry as a whole.

IDEAS THAT WORK

Programming for girls can take place in a short amount of time, such as a trip to the nearby mall, or in a long amount of time, such as a camping trip. Programs can be planned months in advance, like a mother/daughter dinner and talent show, or they can be spontaneous, such as going out for ice cream. Programs can be low cost or no cost, such as driving to a nearby park to watch the sun rise and having a time of prayer, or programs can be more expensive, such as going to an amusement park.

This section is intended to give practical ideas that can be implemented in your ministry. You are encouraged to modify these programs to meet the needs of your girls. Some of the ideas I have personally seen implemented and some have been collected from other women in youth ministries around the country.

The following ideas are just a sample of "girls only" activities that can be sponsored by youth ministries. Youth staff should network with other staff women in the same geographical location to share ideas or even collaborate on several special programs with other youth groups. Many times similar hours are spent organizing a program whether 50 or 100 girls attend. Why not invite girls from another ministry or two to join your group? One of the most rare resources is staff time and availability to implement the ideas. If youth staff will invite other local ministries or individuals to their special events, more girls can benefit from the program, and the guest staff will gratefully appreciate the chance to participate in a quality program that they weren't responsible for executing.

It is important to know the "why" or purpose of the programs planned. The questions you should ask when implementing a program are:

- Why are you offering the program?
- What are the goals you hope to accomplish?
- How is the program addressing the needs of the girls?
- How are you going to do the program?
- Who is your target audience?

Programs shouldn't be done for the sake of filling up a calendar. That's not to say that some activities can't be just for fun and a chance for the group to bond together, as long as that is your goal.

Program planning should also take into account what is happening throughout the entire ministry, because each activity affects other areas of ministry. For instance, girls' programs should not compete with the overall programming goals of the youth ministry. Also, it is recommended, in regards to longer weekend events, that a guy's event be planned to coincide with the girls' event. This is not only because of the value of a conference for young men, but also because the young women who typically hang out with these guys are more likely to attend the conference if their boyfriend or their guy friends are attending a similar conference, and vice versa. Shorter, one-day events are different and, in most instances, can stand on their own as long as the program complements the ministry.

Weekend Conference

The high school group I worked with had been sponsoring coed winter camps for twenty years; it was time for a change. What could be done differently to really have an impact in the lives of students? We decided to try a separate weekend conference for high school men and women at a nearby college. The high school staff women got together to pray and share ideas and vision. Out of this time together emerged a weekend conference, "Redesigning Women."

We decided to organize the weekend like a typical conference with general sessions, seminars, recreation time, etc. Because this was our first attempt at such a conference, it was difficult for the girls to picture what this weekend was all about. "You mean there will be no guys at all . . . for the whole weekend? What are we going to do for the entire weekend?" Before the conference we decided to plan an activity a month for girls only, to show it was possible to have fun without guys. So, in January we planned a beach party. (Indoors . . . even in California it gets cold!) The youth center was decorated with lawn chairs, beach towels, and ice chests with soda. We cranked up the thermostat. We played volleyball, had a live 50s/60s band, ate hot dogs, popsicles, and popcorn. Well, the girls had a blast and realized they could have fun without the opposite sex.

For the most part, all aspects of this conference were organized and run by women, including publicity, planning, facility set-up, running the sound system, etc. I believe the weekend had several benefits over shorter or coed events. First, because the staff spent many hours planning and working together, they bonded quickly, and even new staff felt needed and experienced an immediate sense of belonging. I also observed that the girls who attended didn't worry about impressing any guys, so they ate a lot more food, felt free to be crazy together, got to know other girls in the group, opened up to more thoughtful discussions, allowed themselves to be vulnerable, and enjoyed an environment that allowed God to personally speak to them (staff included)! The following is a summary of some of the components of the conference:

Main sessions included a speaker, music (performed by the women's quartet from our church), personal testimonies by staff women, video clips, and drama sketches. All elements tied in with the message of the session. The speaker(s) were women talking to girls about issues relevant to them. The first year, we brought in an outside speaker to cover issues of friendship, family, fulfillment, and future. The second year, two of our own staff women covered issues dealing with needs and fears; the traps of approval, performance, blame, and shame. Both formats worked well; the success of either option depends on the knowledge and gifts of staff versus the availability and cost of a limited number of women speakers.

For our *Master of Ceremonies* we had two staff dress up and portray different characters to do introductions, crowd breakers, and conduct prize giveaways. The first year we had Helga & Olga from the "old country" who wore long braids and talked in a heavy accent. Another year we had "biker mommas." As a promotional announcement, they rode into the youth center on motorcycles! The students really had fun with the characters and asked for reappearances throughout the year.

Seminars were offered twice during the weekend by women on the high school staff and other women in the church. Past titles include: "Friendships," "A Collection or a Commitment," "Fathers and Daughters," "Who Me? Insecure?," "Beautiful Babes," "Please Understand Me," and "PMS (Pre-Marriage Standards)."

Facilities and Meals were provided by a nearby college. The main sessions, gatherings, and meals were held in the Event Center. Seminars were held in the various meeting rooms and lounges. During free time the game room and convenience store remained open. We slept in the gym and used the showers in the athletic facility. There was no kitchen available, so we had to be creative — delivered pizza, sandwiches, cereal, muffins, fruit, etc. For dinner one year we had an etiquette night at which we learned the proper way to set a table and what to do with all those forks!

Free Time Activities consisted of a variety of activities and games. The college where our conference was held has a game room complete with pool tables, air hockey, Ping-Pong, table soccer, and board games. There was also volleyball, frisbee, and football available depending on the weather. The most popular of our free time activities was Buddy Portraits, where the staff take pictures of the students with their friends. We borrowed costumes and props from the church to create three different theme sets. Staff and students assisted the girls in dressing up, doing hair, and putting on makeup. Girls who have never had anyone help them get "pretty," blossomed with all the attention. The film was taken to a one-hour photo developer so the girls could leave with their buddy portrait.

Special Events consisted of a night game followed by a bonfire. The girls wanted an activity where they could get dirty . . . and have an adventure. The guys had a night game, so they wanted a night game! We played "capture the flag" in the dark. The main point of the game was to run around in the dark, laugh, scream, and fall in the mud. After the game, we had a bonfire at a nearby ranch. We had communion together, sang, shared what we learned during the weekend, and the seniors gave their parting advice to the group. I believe this weekend conference had many of those special "I remember when" moments the girls will remember years from now, and it has become a yearly event for the group.

Grub Camp

Many girls enjoy camping. Grub camp involves taking a group of girls camping or backpacking and roughing it a little. Nothing bonds girls together like having to share a tent together, experiencing a high ropes course, rock climbing, or starting a campfire and making "s'mores." If boys aren't participating, the urge to bring hair dyers, curling irons, and washing machines diminishes (somewhat).

Nights before Christmas

This is an overnight activity that can be held at someone's home or at church. Activities can include watching Christmas movies, baking Christmas cookies, singing Christmas carols to the neighborhood, wrapping up donated toys for homeless children, etc.

Welcome "Freshwomen" Overnighter

This activity can be sponsored/planned by the upcoming seniors or upperclass girls to welcome the new freshmen into the high school group. Moving up from the junior high to the high school group can be intimidating. To assist with the transition and make the new freshmen feel welcome, schedule this activity the weekend of or before the new girls join the high school group. The upperclass girls are responsible for assisting with invitations, food, and activities. When the older girls take ownership for assisting with the transition of the new freshmen, they see their role as "big sister," and the new girls feel wanted and a part of the group.

S.U.R.E. (Servants Uniting for Radical Exaltation)

This is an all-night prayer meeting for high school girls, in which prayer is *experienced* in many different ways. The evening is divided into several segments, each with a different focus. The girls divide up into groups and learn a verse about prayer in sign language, have one word prayers, open-eyed prayer, etc.

Feminar

This is an all-day seminar/conference on "girl things": wardrobe, makeup, aerobics, internal beauty, etc. The Feminar can be held at church, a special conference sight, or at a local health club. For a real conference feel, provide a luncheon and name badges. Also, contact department stores to provide free samples for giveaways to all participants or for door prizes.

Breakfast Club

The Breakfast Club is an early morning Bible study and/or prayer group at a nearby restaurant, donut shop, or home. Bible study topics can vary depending on the needs and desires of the group. One popular topic has been studying women of the Bible.

Outlet Shopping

Choose a day to go to the outlets or malls. Have a crazy goal like how many items can you buy for $5 in half-an-hour. Encourage the girls' mothers to join in and assist in the driving. The drive there and back can be great relational time.

Mother's Day or Special Mother's Appreciation Day

The main idea for this event is the students planning, producing, and participating in a special tribute to mothers (grandmothers, step-mothers,etc.). The event can be scheduled during the youth Sunday School hour at church or at another time. As the mothers arrive, pin a flower on them and maybe even hand out a small gift. Portraits can be taken of mothers and daughters and distributed the following week at church. A meal or even a small snack and beverage can be provided. The program can consist of a speaker, special songs, drama sketches, videos or slides, and a special time for the students to stand up and say what their mom means to them.

Mom and Daughter Bowling League

An activity like bowling can be a popular type of intergenerational activity to bring the young and young at heart together. Each team is made up of a woman and a girl (i.e., grandmothers, mothers and daughters, big and little sisters, etc.). Each pair competes against other partners or teams and can conclude with a tournament.

Spa Night

This is a great alternative to a lock-in. Have the girls give each other facials and manicures. Obtain some free samples from local cosmetic counters. Rent a hot tub. Talk about the book of Esther. Eat and wear health food.

Mother/Daughter Activities

There are a variety of activities that can be shared by groups of mothers and daughter, such as, facials, shopping, and plays.

Mentor Moms

Mentor Moms is part of a larger ministry called, "Special Care" at First Baptist Church in Modesto, California. The purpose of

Mentor Moms is to match Christian women with teen mothers or mothers-to-be in order to provide spiritual, emotional, and physical support for the teen mother and her baby.

The recognition of the need for this ministry arose from seeing the increasing number of teen moms in the community. While most middle-class girls are choosing abortion, those in lower socioeconomic groups are keeping and raising their babies. They have few or no role models or emotional support. Many come from backgrounds of sexual and physical abuse and neglect. Most have no spiritual upbringing and do not know the love of Jesus. They will continue their promiscuous lifestyle in a desperate search for love. They and their babies are doomed to a life of poverty, sexually transmitted diseases, and more abuse. We cannot say, "Don't have abortions, be a good mom . . . " and not reach out in love to a lost generation of teen girls. As a Special Care mentoring mom, women can be the bridge of hope to a new life that will continue to affect future generations.

Sisters Inc. (In Christ)
Sisters Inc. is an outreach program that helps bring young, pregnant girls into the regular youth ministry, meet their need for understanding and friendship, and model for them the life God has planned for them. Christian teen girls are matched one-to-one with a pregnant teen or teen mother in order to provide friendship and acceptance into the high school ministry and into other activities.

Adopt a Little Sister or Two
High school girls can be paired with younger girls within the church or local community. Once paired up, the big sister can go to her little sister's soccer games, get involved as a tutor, invite her to go grocery shopping, etc. After earning her trust and confidence a big sister can truly be a Christian role model for her younger sister.

Discipleship Ideas for Women Youth Leaders and Girls
Youth workers agree on the importance of discipling today's youth, but what is the difference, if any, between discipling guys

and girls? Girls are typically more relational and enjoy getting together to talk, discuss feelings, etc. Guys, on the other hand, are typically not as relational and normally find it more difficult and even uncomfortable talking in groups. It is much easier for men to develop relationships and talk if it's during or including an activity such as sports, fishing, etc.

Discipleship Groups

Women discipling girls is a very powerful way to multiply and pass on a living Christian faith to future generations. It is impossible to measure the effects that discipling a young believer has and will have. We may only know when we get to heaven. Out of discipleship groups mentor relationships can develop. These relationships take time and normally can only occur with a few students at a time. Discipleship can take place in different forms within a youth group. The following briefly describes some the these different combinations.

Staff to Students

Staff discipling students is probably what we think of first when we think of discipleship occurring in a youth ministry. Staff can disciple mature Christian students or new believers on a one-to-one basis or as part of a small group.

Some youth groups set up discipleship groups as young women become Christians. Discipleship for new believers can take place in small groups or on a one-on-one basis, providing special opportunities for nurturing, mentoring, and discipleship.

A Day of Parables

A Day of Parables is a one day event in which a staff person meets with a small group of girls to facilitate a special time of learning together. The staff person shouldn't lecture or teach but instead give them a focus for the day and provide them with a small notebook to write down ideas they get during the day. Several experiences can be provided, such as sitting on the roof of a building (approved, of course), putting together a puzzle without the lid/picture, and cooking an edible meal with diverse ingredients and no recipe. The girls can pull out some incredible truths. The day then ends with a time of sharing. An example is exploring a graveyard and talking about what lasts in life or going to an art institute and finding a work of art that best describes how God wired you.

Students to Students

Older girls can be matched with younger girls to support, encourage, and pray together. For many of the older girls, discipling a younger student is the first time they see others looking up to them in a leader/young adult role. Discipling another girl might be the first experience of being responsible for another person. Staff can assist in the developing of leaders by meeting with these older girls to offer leadership and discipling training.

Prayer triplets are made of three students that meet before school or during the lunch hour. These prayer groups are not Bible studies, but a time to pray, share, and encourage one another.

*   *   *

Yes, we believe that there is a place for same gender activities in youth ministries, but don't feel as if you have to limit your creativity by just using our suggestions. Try a few of your own, and let us know about the ones that are especially successful.

A special thanks to the student ministries staff at First Baptist Church in Modesto, California, and especially Marilyn Jones and Cheryl Jacobo, Jean Tippitt from Christ UMC in Mobile, Alabama, Melinda Schluckebier from Calvary Lutheran Church, in Elgin, Illinois, and Tricia Murphy and Jana Sundene from "Student Impact" high school ministry of Willow Creek Community Church in South Barrington, Illinois.

BARRIER BREAKERS

1. How would the girls in your ministry benefit from a girls only program?

2. What kind of program do the girls in your ministry need? (Service project, community building time, spiritual refreshment . . .)

3. What are your resources for an all-girls event?

4. What are additional ideas for all-girl activities?

Author

Name: *Karen Grant*

Occupation: *Women's Coordinator for student ministries at First Evangelical Free Church in Rockford, Illinois*

Birthplace: *San Mateo, California*

Marital status: *Single . . . still looking*

Kids: *My two Shelties, "Marriott" and "Rudy"*

The last movie that significantly impacted me was: Shadowlands

A good book I would recommend is: *This one!*

If I weren't in youth ministry, I'd be: *Teaching at a college*

I love to: *Attend live theatrical productions, especially musicals*

One thing I could live without ever doing again is: *Writing another thesis*

In my lifetime I still want to: *Go on a short-term missions trip to a different country*

I don't really like: *Lima beans*

One of my passions is to: *Train and care for animals*

People always think I'm: *Younger than I really am*

I've learned that: *Life on earth is short. Don't get stressed out with daily hassles. Keep your focus on God.*

I would like to encourage my colleagues to: *Train and support younger women interested in youth ministry*

I would like to be remembered for: *Being a women of integrity who followed God's will for her life*

TWELVE

Helping Girls Who Hurt
Invervention for girls in crisis

by Saundra Hensel with Terryl Overpeck, MA, LMST

When I met Paige for the first time, she was fifteen years old. Although she was young, Paige had been pegged as a leader in our high school ministry from the time she first got involved. Now we were both volunteers. She had a sense of fun and excitement that was incredibly contagious. Despite the fact that I was two years older, we became close friends as we both grew in our leadership. Together, we served in the ministry to disciple girls and bring newcomers to Christ. Our friendship grew as well. We spent countless hours on the phone, talking over pizza, praying, and laughing together. Then one day came the news that Paige had been admitted to an adolescent psychiatric unit in a hospital following a suicide attempt. I learned that the laughter, fun, and even her service to the ministry had hidden a life of sexual abuse, bulimia, chemical dependence, and despair.

Over the subsequent years of our friendship, there has been no greater pain for me than the fact that I didn't see what was happening, and, as a result, didn't support Paige in the way she needed. I never asked the question that needed to be asked, never saw the signs and signals she was sending. Just recently, she confessed to me that during that early time, she needed support from me, but didn't feel that she could tell me the truth about everything that had happened to her. So she lied and told me she'd had an abortion, feeling that was more acceptable than what was really going on with her. It was only after a long period of time that she was able to tell me the truth. Today, Paige has come to a place in her life where she is working hard to find healing emotionally, physically, and spiritually. As a result of her growth toward healing, we've spent some time talking about what leaders in the ministry could have done that would have helped her; what they could have seen and questioned. While I don't live in guilt dwelling on what I should have done, I have spent time thinking about it, knowing that I could learn valuable lessons from that experience.

The time to learn what to do when a girl is in crisis is not at the moment she confides in you; it's now. It would be impossible in one chapter (or even a whole book!) to cover in depth all of the information regarding the tough issues girls face today, so I'm not even attempting to say that, after reading this, you can handle any crisis with confidence. When I asked Paige what she would have liked me or another leader in our ministry to do during her early years of crisis, she said, "Just know enough to see the signs and ask the tough questions. *I didn't tell anyone because no one asked.*" My prayer is that this chapter will point you in the right direction as you educate yourself about these issues and also that it will give you some general, guiding principles for future crises.

PREPARING FOR CRISES

To do to make sure you are ready when a student comes to you in crisis, you must first educate yourself. Go to your local bookstore or library and find books about adolescents and the issues they face. Read articles and journals, listen to the news, listen to your students talk; generally, become a student of your students. By watching and listening to the world around you, you will know what the crises are likely to be, and you will know what you need to target in your own research. Keep in tune, as well, to what the rising issues are in your students' culture. When I was in high school, there were girls that would not eat, or would make themselves throw up after eating, but eating disorders weren't a major issue. Now, it's almost an accepted practice among students, and definitely something you need to know about. Fifteen years ago, if you were doing suburban ministry, you didn't really have to worry too much about gangs or drugs. Today, your students face choices about those issues daily. You don't need to be — and never will become — an expert on all adolescent crises. Be wise in choosing those which you think your students will most likely be dealing with and focus your education on those.

A second way to prepare yourself is through knowing your resources. Does your church host any twelve-step groups? Is there a counseling center in your community that specializes in adolescent treatment? What hospitals have adolescent psychiatric units? Most of us in student ministries aren't professional counselors and aren't qualified to provide any more care for a family in crisis than support, encouragement, and help in finding professional help for them; therefore, it's important that you meet with some counselors in your area. Get to know them, their style of treatment, and any specialties they may have. Put them on your referral list. If you recommend counseling to a family, always give them a couple of names, that way the choice is theirs. It's good to have both male and female counselors on your referral list. Keep in mind that most issues go beyond just the student and affect the family, so it's also a good idea to know counselors who are qualified family counselors, not just adolescent counselors.

Finally, and probably the most important to your own health, is to build a support network for yourself. Have a professional counselor or two whom you can call when you need advice on where to go with a situation. Sometimes you may not be sure how to handle a crisis, if you should refer, if you should involve the parents, or if you can and should deal with the situation yourself. Being able to call a professional at this point for advice can take the pressure off of you, so you don't feel as if you are making decisions in vacuum. Find someone to bounce ideas off.

Another part of your formal network will probably be the youth pastor if you're a volunteer or the senior pastor if you're on staff. Who is the person to whom you need to report major incidents? You need to have someone else in the church know what action you are taking and give you feedback on situations. Find out who that person should be for you.

A more informal network can also be helpful. If you have a

friend who is a counselor or a relationship with another youth worker in the area who has experience with students in crisis, these are people who can also give good advice and feedback.

One way in which I've found my network to be invaluable is in affirming actions and decisions I've made. While preparing this chapter, I received a phone call from a mother whose oldest son is completely out of control. That evening I talked to Terryl, the counselor who gave me professional input on this chapter. I told her about my conversation with the mother and the advice I'd given. It helped me tremendously to hear Terryl affirm my advice and tell me that it was sound. Informal and formal networks are a vital part of being prepared for serving students in crisis.

Once you've established your network, educated yourself on key issues, and found out what your resources are, you can have confidence that you have prepared yourself well for students in crisis.

SIGNS OF CRISIS

Each of the crisis issues this chapter will cover has its own symptoms that are unique to that issue and will be discussed in the individual section. There are, however, some general signs that you can observe which will give you a good indication that there could be something disturbing going on in the student's life and it would be a good idea to approach the student. Remember, the earlier you can spot a potential crisis, the better off the student will be.

First, observe the student physically. This can be difficult because grunge is such a fashion, but if a student who has tended to dress moderately or at least in a clean, neat style, starts to wear sloppy, stained, or torn clothes, it could be a sign of a disturbance in her life. Also in terms of physical appearance, notice the student's personal hygiene. A student in crisis will usually become careless in caring for themselves. Does it seem as if she hasn't showered? Is her hair greasy? Does he have an overall disheveled appearance? Finally, if you see unusual bruising or even scratches and signs of self-mutilation, you should intervene as soon as possible.

Another category of signs to look for is sudden changes of behavior or personality. A girl who tends to be pretty mellow suddenly becomes almost manic. The "life of the party" begins to sit by herself during youth group and doesn't show up for activities. An easygoing type becomes defensive and angry. Sudden changes may also occur in grades and performance. A student may drop sports, and begin to receive detentions and failing grades. You may notice that a student suddenly has a whole new group of friends and doesn't hang out with her old group anymore. All of these symptoms can be signs of a problem.

Finally, listen to what the student and others around her are saying. While most signs are non-verbal, there can also be some signs that are verbal. A student may suddenly begin talking inappropriately, swearing, talking tough, or lying. Other students may talk about the girl, giving clues such as, "What's up with Rachel? She just sits home all the time and never wants to do anything anymore."

Watching and listening will supply you with the information you need to begin a conversation. Write down what you've seen, heard, and noticed. Then set up a time to talk with the student and try to discover if there is a crisis or potential crisis in her life.

APPROACHING THE STUDENT

Observing behaviors and changes in the student is the easy part; talking to the student is the hard part. First, decide if you are the one who should actually meet with the student. Is there another leader in the ministry who has a closer relationship with the girl? If so, talk to that leader to see if she has seen the same things. Compare notes and decide if it would be more appropriate for the other leader to meet with the student. If you haven't earned the girl's trust through a relationship, the chances of her opening up to you are slim.

When you meet with the student, make sure it's a safe, private environment. Going to her house, where her brother might walk in the room won't make her feel very comfortable. Neither will pulling her aside during the youth group in front of all her friends. She knows they will ask her later what you wanted, so she's not going to tell you anything she isn't willing to repeat to her friends. You also should make sure that you have plenty of time. You may meet with her at 3:30 P.M., find out she's being sexually abused by her father, and realize you aren't going to have time to call your advisory committee to tell them you won't be able to meet at 4 P.M. If you really suspect there is something serious going on, be sure to build flex time into your schedule to deal with it right then, if needed. In addition, students can usually tell if you are pressed for time and this will inhibit them.

Begin your conversation by sharing your observations. It is very important that you don't interpret what you've seen. Don't say, "I've noticed that you have started talking very sexually lately. That's often a sign of someone being sexually abused. What's going on?" You don't want to plant ideas in her head or ask leading questions. Simply state your observations without interpretation. "Your mom mentioned your grades have slipped this semester, and I've noticed you don't seem to be able to focus during our small group time. Is something bothering you?"

When the student begins to explain her behavior, whether or not she is truthful and opens up at this point, the most important thing you can do is *be a good listener.* Try to hear behind what she is saying, so you can follow up with deeper questions. Actively listening will also help her to develop more trust in your relationship.

If the student is in a crisis of some kind, then you can proceed to deal with it in the appropriate manner. If she gives an explanation that shows you she is just going through a normal, adolescent stage of confusion, you can help get her on the way to working through that rough spot. The hardest alternative for me, however, is when the student doesn't express any kind of crisis, yet the pat answer she gives as an explanation, her apology for her behavior, even her promise to change, just don't ring true. There are times when my gut says there's more to the story than I'm hearing. At that point, it's OK to share that feeling. Again, be careful not to lead or plant ideas, but be free to state your impression. "I'm not really convinced that there isn't more to this. I want you to know that I'm willing to listen if you decide you'd like to share more with me. I do hope if something is going on, that you will talk to someone about it." Leave the door open for her to talk to you, encourage her to talk to someone, but understand that you can't make a person want to get help. The choice is hers.

Once the meeting is over, document the conversation. Write down any explanations she gave and any steps she committed to take. Keeping this kind of documentation can be of great help and protection, to you and her, if the crisis escalates.

CONFIDENTIALITY

The cardinal rule about confidentiality is never, ever to promise it. That way, you know you'll never have to break that promise. If you do tell a student you won't tell anyone, and it ends up that you have to in order to protect her, you risk losing all credibility with the kids in your ministry. They don't care that it was important to share the information, they just care that you broke a promise. If a girl asks you to promise confidentiality, say, "I can't promise that. I hope that if you trust me enough to confide in me, you trust me enough to act responsibly with the information you give me. I can promise that I won't tell anyone without talking to you about it first, and that I won't tell anyone I feel doesn't have an absolute need to know."

Parent Involvement

The big question for youth workers is often *if* and *when* to talk to parents. The lines are pretty clearly drawn in situations where the student's life or welfare are involved, like suicide, abuse, or advanced eating disorders. But what about the student who is experimenting with alcohol or drugs? The main strategy is to encourage the student herself to talk to her parents. In the real world however, the one most of us live in, the student is not going to tell her parents. The most effective way to handle the more ambiguous situations, then, is to set clear boundaries for the times when you have responsibility for the student. Make sure to let her know the consequences for breaking the boundaries during your time together, one of which being that there will be discussion with her parents. She needs to know that she can't come to youth group high or smelling of alcohol, or that she can't purge on retreats. The key is to clearly define acceptable behavior and appropriate consequences. Then, if boundaries are broken, she can only be angry with herself for making poor choices.

UNDERSTANDING THE NATURE OF THE CRISIS

Knowing potential crisis situations is part of your preparation for responding appropriately to crises. The following list of issues is by no means exhaustive, nor are the descriptions and suggestions meant to be a complete education in themselves. Hopefully, what follows will give you a good foundation on which to build as the need arises.

Eating Disorders

There are three common forms of eating disorders in adolescents: anorexia nervosa, bulimia, and overeating. While eating disorders are not exclusive to girls, they are definitely more common in girls. A core issue for girls who develop an eating disorder is control. Their home environment may be one of either chaos or rigid control. They view eating as something that they are able to control, either in the midst of chaos or when everything else in their life is being controlled by others.

Another aspect of eating disorders is the secondary gains they often bring. Food can temporarily feel comforting and soothing. Or, if girls lose weight, they're told by others how good they look which brings a major boost in their self-esteem. For Christian students especially, an eating disorder may seem acceptable. Drugs are illegal, they know sex is a sin, but food is neutral so they don't see their eating disorder as a problem.

Signs and Solutions. Anorexia nervosa is voluntary starvation or rigid dieting that leads to rapid, dramatic weight loss. Students who are anorexic may exhibit signs such as: obsessive interest in food, perfectionism, withdrawing, maintaining rigid control, excessive exercise, depression, irritability, and food rituals. Also, menstrual periods may stop, and students may say they are fat even when emaciated. When confronted, the anorexic most often denies there is a problem. It's important to confront the student with very direct observations and questions. If the student isn't willing to admit the problem and you perceive it as life threatening, you need to talk to her parents. Anorexia can lead to death.

Bulimia is a binging and purging syndrome. Following a time of excessive eating, the student will take laxatives or induce vomiting to purge herself of the food. Bulimics tend to be within ten to fifteen pounds of their ideal body weight, so weight loss isn't as much of a sign for this disorder. Signs for bulimia include: secretive behavior regarding eating, irregular periods, broken blood vessels in face, fainting spells, swollen glands in neck, loss of tooth enamel, desiring relationships with and the approval of others, and the actual binging and purging.

Like anorexics, bulimics have a root problem with control. As they slide further into their eating disorder, however, they begin to realize that they are being controlled by the binging and purging and are more likely than anorexics to admit the problem and ask for help. Again, the key approach involves direct questions, knowing that bulimia can also be a life threatening problem.

Depression/Suicide

The core issue for students who experience severe depression or are suicidal is hopelessness. The adolescent culture and mindset today tends toward hopelessness anyway, but for the depressed/suicidal student, there is a deeper hopelessness, usually triggered by a recent situation in her life. It could be a death or any kind of loss; a breakup, a divorce, moving, a pet's death. Whatever the cause, depression needs to be taken very seriously, simply because it often will lead to a suicide attempt.

Signs and Solutions. Students who are depressed and considering suicide will often exhibit sudden changes in their eating habits and their personality. They may begin dropping out of activities, sports, and relationships, becoming preoccupied with death. Their grades may begin to drop, and they might give away their possessions. All of these are cause for concern and action. However, if the student has attempted suicide before, or there is a family history of suicide, she may need more immediate help. The major warning flags in depressed students can help identify those at risk of suicide.

When approaching a depressed student you believe might be suicidal, ask the question directly. "Have you considered killing or hurting yourself in any way?" Suicidal students tend to be honest about what they're experiencing. By phrasing the question in a way that's broader than just killing themselves, you open the door for them to tell you if they've had thoughts about driving recklessly, smashing into a tree, or other destructive behavior. Try to determine if her thoughts are a way of expressing pain or a serious thought of suicide. Does she have a plan? Does she have access to pills or a gun? Determine if the student is actively suicidal or asking for help. Don't get into a debate about suicide — she is not having a rational response to her pain, so you will not win a rational argument.

If the student is actively suicidal, meaning she might leave your office and go make an attempt, take immediate action. *Don't leave her alone.* If you need to leave to call her parents, get someone else to come in the room and stay with her. Also, don't drive her home yourself. You don't want a suicidal girl in your car as you're driving 55 mph on the highway. Have her parents come and get her so they can bring her somewhere for evaluation and treatment. If necessary, you can call the police.

If the student is not actively suicidal, meaning she is having thoughts about it, but there isn't a whole lot of danger that she's going to leave your office and kill herself immediately, affirm her for talking to you about the problem and assure her that you will try to help. Then, work with her to explore other alternatives to suicide and the consequences of the alternatives. Avoid giving advice, but help her to problem solve and develop some short-term goals. This will help give her a sense of hope and progress. Also help her identify a few other people she can confide in and talk to when she starts to feel overwhelmed; help her develop a support network. Preferably, at least one of those people should be an adult. Before she leaves, get a commitment from her that she won't hurt herself or attempt suicide for three days and that during that time she will talk to her parents and get professional help. Set up a tangible plan for a future meeting after those three days, and get a commitment from her that she will be at that meeting. Document your meeting and follow-up plan.

Substance Abuse

The core issue for students involved in substance abuse is escape. They are unhappy with their life and the world, and drugs and alcohol help to deaden the pain. Unfortunately, it's no longer unusual for students to experiment with drugs and alcohol. With drugs widely available even in grade schools, it's no wonder that substance use and abuse in students is on the rise. For youth workers, the issue of substance abuse can be tricky. You are not a detective and you cannot control what the student does at school or at home. This is where setting boundaries within your sphere of influence is crucial. With careful planning, clearly defined boundaries, and follow-through, you can influence what students do and don't do during meetings, retreats, and activities.

Signs and Solutions. The signs of a student who is involved in substance abuse include some signs listed previously for students in crisis: an obvious change in friends, drop in grades, personality changes, withdrawal from activities, poor attitude toward authority, and apathetic or disoriented behavior. In addition, substance abusers will often show an increased need for money and become dishonest. Being stoned, drunk, or having drug paraphernalia are some of the more obvious signs.

Documentation and observation are important before you approach the student. Then, state your observations and any facts you know. If the student admits to using drugs or alcohol, ask direct questions. How long has she used them? How often and how much? Do her parents know? Be sure to label what she is doing as illegal. While most know drugs are illegal, many students don't really think about the fact that it is illegal for them to drink. If they are involved in your ministry, they probably have some sensitivity to spiritual matters, so ask them what they are going to do about the fact that they are involved in illegal activity. Are they willing to stop? Are they willing to discuss it with their parents? Continue to follow up with them and be firm with the boundaries and consequences you've set.

Physical or Sexual Abuse

The core issue for students who are being abused is shame. They often blame themselves for the abuse. "If I were a better daughter, Mom wouldn't hit me." Or "I've done something to make Uncle Bob want to have sex with me." Or, "It's my fault that Uncle Bob wants to have sex with me." This shame issue makes abuse hard to identify and very difficult for a student to confide.

Signs and Solutions. Students who are being abused, either physically or sexually, tend to become very secretive. They often develop other crises to help them escape from the very painful issue of abuse. This means that substance abuse, eating disorders, depression, and even suicidal tendencies can be a way they cope with abuse. Abused students will usually withdraw, but sometimes they can become very aggressive. Excessive bruises, broken bones, and an abnormal amount of "accidents" can be a sign of physical abuse. A student who begins talking in a way that is inappropriately crude and very sexually explicit may be being sexually abused.

When approaching the student, share your observations. If the student tells you she is being abused, get some of the general details. Who is abusing her? Is it sexual or physical? Is the abuse still going on? When did the last incident take place? Has she told anyone else? You don't need to know all the details, but you do need to know enough to make an informed decision. Give her choices in terms of how to handle the situation. This is especially important because she's in a situation where she feels she has no choice. Her parents (the non-abusive one if one of them is the abuser) need to be told. Does she want to tell them alone, or does she want you to be with her? It's important that you know the laws of your state regarding your responsibility to report abuse and to consult with someone else knowledgeable about abuse situations before making a report. Walk through the situation with your pastor or a counselor. The ideal situation is to get the student to a counselor. As a professional, he or she can make the call regarding if the abuse needs to be reported to the authorities. Don't handle an abuse issue on your own. Whatever steps you end up taking, make sure to document the conversations and processes.

One of the questions and fears in everyone's minds regarding abuse is, what if the student is lying? Kids can get very angry at their parents and may decide that claiming abuse would make a great form of revenge. And in that circumstance you become a manipulation tool. To guard yourself against that, make sure to listen for holes in the student's story and see if it rings true. However, the rule of thumb is that abuse is a serious issue and deserves to be taken seriously. So don't doubt a student unless you have good reason. It is good to get the student into the hands of a professional as soon as possible; they are trained in discerning the real issues. Our responsibility is to protect children; therefore, it's better to err on the side of protecting them rather than ignoring the problem.

Sexual Issues

Probably the most common crisis issues you will face fall into the area of sexual issues: pregnancy, abortion, and sexually transmitted diseases. Since this is such a common issue, the following chapter is devoted to dealing with these complex topics.

ON THE WAY TO HEALING

As a youth worker, even though I feel that I've prepared myself to deal with student crises, my heart still drops into my stomach when a student walks up to me with "that look" in her eyes and says, "I really need to talk to you." My prayer for you is that when you are approached like that, or when you recognize the signs and you approach a student, you will know you've done what you can to be prepared to walk her through the tough issues and find healing and growth.

BARRIER BREAKERS

1. **What are the current issues your students are dealing with?**

2. **Do you have ministry procedures for dealing with a student in crisis?**

3. What crisis training have you or your team had?

4. Do you have a crisis network that you can access? If not, what specific topics do you need to address?

Author

Name: *Saundra Hensel*
Occupation: Student Ministries Director at Cedar Ridge Community Church
Current home: Maryland
My favorite food is: Pizza and Diet Dr. Pepper
The last movie that significantly impacted me was: *Lady Jane*
The style that best reflects me is: Contemporary
If I could do it over: I'd graduate from college in less than 10 years
If I could change one thing about myself: I'd be artistic
If I weren't in youth ministry, I'd be: Teaching British literature at a college
Words that best describe me: Funny, thinking, pithy
I love to: Read
I really don't care for: Mushrooms and seafood
If I could go anywhere in the world, it would be: England or Palestine
My favorite pet is: My cat, Pookie
It really bugs me when: People tell me I'll want to get married "when the right man comes along"
The thing that I love about youth ministry is: Camps and retreats
One thing that I could live without ever doing again is: Being strip-searched by airport security in Israel
If I could live anywhere in the world, it would be: A loft in Manhattan or Georgetown (D.C.)
My favorite place to spend time with God is: On a mountain or by the ocean
One of my passions is to: See Broadway shows
I've learned that: I shouldn't take myself or life too seriously
I would like to be remembered for: Helping people enjoy God and life a little more

THIRTEEN

When Bandages Aren't Enough
Addressing the sexual issues of girls

by Nancy Sanders

It was early in the evening when I admitted a pretty, seventeen-year-old girl into her hospital room. Her gait was awkward as she climbed into the bed, but her smile was pleasant, and she appeared comfortable as I began the admission interview. The teen explained that she had been experiencing numbness and tingling in her legs for the past several days, making it difficult to get around. While she was somewhat concerned about the possible causes of this problem, she was more concerned about getting out of the hospital in time to begin college in just a few days. The interview continued, and when I came to the section concerning sexual history, she stated that she was not currently sexually active, although she had had one sexual encounter several months prior, which she now regretted. She further revealed that her partner had worn a condom.

In the hours following, many blood tests were done, and while many diseases were ruled out, one test came back positive: herpes. The days that followed were difficult, as intravenous medication had to be given to curtail the virus, which had apparently affected her central nervous system. What was difficult for me, however, was watching this young girl anguish over telling her parents about the one night which had resulted in a disease she would carry with her for the rest of her life. I will never forget seeing the tears in her eyes as she said to me, "It's not fair. I did everything I was supposed to do to protect myself. So why did this happen?"

As the chapter title indicates, students today are suffering from ailments that the superficial Band-Aid our society offers cannot begin to cure. In the sexual arena today we are seeing victims in epidemic proportions. A staggering percentage of youth today, even churched youth, are making the decision to become involved sexually, the consequences of which we have only just begun to see. Teenagers today have more sexually transmitted diseases than any other age group, with an estimated 2.5 million cases in this country alone.[1] The number of people with Acquired Immune Deficiency Syndrome (AIDS) has reached 1 million and is doubling every 2.8 years. Some studies indicate that at least 20 percent of those with AIDS were infected as teenagers.[2] Forty percent of 14 year olds today will become pregnant by the time they are 19, according to current trends.[3] Sexual crimes committed against teens are also increasing, as is our awareness that these evils really do exist. The largest study of sexual assault on college campuses indicates that a woman's risk of sexual assault is approximately 25 percent.[4] Unfortunately, the horrors of sexual abuse have even entered the home, where thousands of cases of sexual molestation and incest are reported yearly. There should be little doubt in anyone's mind that teenagers today have a tremendous need for healing.

As health care and insurance coverage are debated by our government and by individuals, "preventative medicine" has become a familiar term in most circles. By treating the predisposing factors before the illness occurs, much discomfort, heartache, and money can be saved. So it is with youth ministry, particularly when the lives of the teens are on the line—as they are with so many sexual issues. While many parents are actively involved in "preventative" measures with their teens, many more are taking a passive role in the education of their children. Not coincidentally, the public school system is taking up the slack left by parents and "educating" children in an effort to turn around the alarming statistics. These controversial "morally neutral" programs have done little to decrease the pregnancy rates or the spread of disease among our youth. Thus, as youth leaders, we are left with no other choice but to add the role of "sex educator" to our long list of responsibilities. As women, we can empathize with girls struggling with their sexuality, we can draw on already established relationships as we discuss sensitive issues, and we can add a broader perspective to the entire curriculum when working with mixed groups of students. While often a difficult task, it can blend beautifully with our firm desire to teach teens about God's best for their lives.

As a busy mother, nurse, and youth leader, I enjoy books that have that cut-to-the-quick practicality that I can read and put into practice at the next youth meeting. So, how does the woman in youth ministry design a curriculum to prevent sexual involvement and its consequences? Here are some guidelines.

EDUCATE YOURSELF

Christian bookstores and youth worker catalogs are filled with hundreds of resources that can give you lesson ideas, statistics, and facts you can use to teach the truth about sex to your group. Ministries such as "Why Wait?" by Josh McDowell and Focus on the Family provide excellent audio and videotapes along with wonderfully written materials to help you clarify the message that teens need to hear.

GET THE PARENTS INVOLVED

The media, the schools, and often peers are influencing youth to do what "feels right." We need support on our side, and parents can be a strong asset for the youth leader. Even though students are pressured by many outside forces, parental attitudes about sex still directly shape the attitudes of their children. Also, because of the nature of the subject matter, parents appreciate being included in the curriculum choices and lessons. Just as youth groups vary, however, the parents will differ in how involved they want to be. It is best to leave them some space. Send a letter to parents before you begin (or have a meeting, if you have a high level of involvement) to outline exactly what you will be teaching. Encourage parents to contact you with any questions or concerns. Explain that you will provide them with opportunities to get involved with what their teens are learning in the weeks to come. I have found in most cases that parents are happy to have their teen involved and appreciate the "help" in communicating with their teen about uncomfortable issues. Once the lessons begin, periodically send home some questions for the students to discuss with their parents. This can help teens learn what their parents think about topics like dating, how to deal with sexual pressure, and how to build trust. The following week, ask students to discuss how effectively they communicated with their parents, or if they even did at all. This can be a valuable learning experience.

PREPARE TO BE FRANK

When discussing the physical risks of sexually transmitted diseases (pain, infertility, cervical cancer, etc.), your message will be less effective if you blush with every anatomical term or appear uncomfortable with the subject matter. While it is not necessary or even wise to be overly graphic, tell it like it is. Chances are, the students are hearing much worse in their health class at school.

BE POSITIVE

Just as preaching the Gospel is more than "fire and brimstone," teaching about the value of abstinence is more than just disease and pregnancy prevention. Talk to your group about how abstinence keeps one from confusing sex with love, how it allows trust in a marriage, and develops self-control. Share with them that sex is from God and that He designed it for our enjoyment when we use it according to His plan.

TEACH THEM HOW TO SAY NO

"Just say no" stands little chance against peer pressure and hormones. Describe scenarios that involve sexual pressure and have them role-play how they would handle themselves. Teach them about the difference between male and female sex drives and how this impacts the dating relationship. Discuss potentially dangerous dating circumstances (parking, movies, etc.) and have them brainstorm suggestions for possible locations for dates that would make them more accountable.

BE CREATIVE

Even though this topic tends to draw the largest crowd to your youth meetings, teens will retain more if they get involved. Encourage teens to think of reasons to save sex for marriage and write them on the wall in the church basement (on paper, of course). Have them draw pictures of their dreams for the future, then discuss how sexual involvement could change those dreams. Have a mock game show with questions on sexually transmitted diseases and other consequences . . . anything to get the group thinking!

ROLE MODEL HEALTHY SEXUALITY

Whether married or single, share with the teens, as appropriate, about how God has helped you to follow His plan for your sexuality. Share your struggles; let them know that it isn't easy but it is worth the wait. If you have experienced God's forgiveness in this area, tell them about it if your group is mature enough. It's very possible that forgiveness for sexual sin is something one or more of the teens need to hear about more than anything else.

One of the reasons I like math is because it always works — one plus one always equals two. Unfortunately, as in medicine, prevention does not always prevent illness, and treatment does not always lead to a cure. Teenagers are not an exact science, and it is more than likely that despite a well-planned and executed abstinence curriculum, one or more students in your group will become sexually active or experience the consequences of their prior sexual activity. This lesson was brought home to me last year when I got a phone call from the father of one of the girls in my youth group. She was pregnant and he wanted to know if the church could pay for an abortion. After a quick prayer I set up a meeting with them so my husband and I could discuss this with them further. I hung up the phone, got down on my knees, and cried. The months that followed were difficult, and the story did not end the way I would have liked it to. However, I did glean from that experience some ideas about how to help a student in crisis, whether it is a result of her own decision to get involved sexually or a result of sexual abuse.

DON'T BLAME YOURSELF

Women in youth ministry are particularly vulnerable to blame, as we tend to struggle with self-esteem while trying to maintain our "superwoman" role. Thoughts like, "I should have seen it coming" or "I should have spent more time individually with her" will paralyze you and keep you from meeting the teen's current needs. Being in this situation has given me a small glimpse of how our Heavenly Father feels when we are disobedient. He gave us the guidelines and then lovingly gave us the freedom to choose our path, responding with love no matter which we choose.

UTILIZE YOUR RESOURCES

The youth worker's role in working with teens in crisis should primarily be that of an intermediary, ideally, helping the teen and family to deal with the problem and find the resources they need to do so. Contact your senior pastor or other church leader to which you are accountable for guidance. For a pregnant teen, a local church-affiliated crisis pregnancy center can be a wonderful resource for the youth worker. Whether you contact the center or have the teen do so, be available if the teen or family would like you to join them for the first meeting to ease their anxiety. A teen who confides in you that she has been raped or abused in some way needs to see a professional counselor who can help her deal with the many psychological issues she may face as well. Help her to find an appropriate counselor, using church funds if necessary, and be a support person throughout the counseling. Most youth workers, particularly volunteers, need to realize that our responsibility is to show teens Christ through us, not try to solve all a teen's problems without outside help.

TO TELL OR NOT TO TELL

This classic youth worker's dilemma gets more complicated when it involves sexual issues. In the case of pregnancy, most states consider minors to be emancipated from their parents, and, thus, they can receive testing and treatment without permission from their parents. Testing for sexually transmitted diseases can also be done without parental consent, but treatment requires consent in most states. While it is advisable in almost all cases to encourage a teen to tell her parents, state laws protect her right of privacy. On the other hand, if abuse is suspected, it is your responsibility to notify proper authorities, most likely your area child welfare department. Before doing this, however, discuss the situation in confidence with your pastor or other church leadership. The teen herself is also able to report sexual abuse to the police or child welfare department, but will probably need your support as she takes this difficult step.

NEVER STOP LOVING

In the midst of crisis, teens can make unwise decisions — even decisions that have serious consequences for their life or the life of another. While it is important that we make our feelings clear in light of God's standards, it is also crucial that we demonstrate His love and forgiveness as we spend time with teens. Let them know that no matter what they do, you will never stop caring. After all, that's what Christ does for us!

What an awesome responsibility we have as women working with girls that so desperately need to experience the healing that only the Lord Jesus can give! As you endeavor to practice some prevention and treatment with the teens you minister to, never forget that the most important thing you can do for them is give them to God in prayer. When bandages aren't enough, aren't you glad the Doctor is in?

BARRIER BREAKERS

1. What resources/education do you need to add to your "library" or network to better equip your ministry?

2. What is your ministry doing to better equip parents, students, and leaders on this topic?

3. Who are the local speakers who can effectively communicate with your students on this topic?

4. What is your organization's policy on dealing with students who face a sexual crisis?

Author

Name: *Nancy Sanders*

Occupation: *Registered nurse, mom, housewife, and volunteer youth worker*
Current home: *Des Plaines, Illinois*
Marital status: *Married*
Children: *Scott (1)*
My favorite food is: *Pizza*
Favorite childhood memory: *My dad would sit next to me as he tucked me into bed, and we would talk about whatever I wanted to talk about. He listened to me and made me feel valued*
Nobody knows I'm: *Frequently stressed out! Many people seem to think that I have it all together, which is not always the case!*
I'm working on: *Prioritizing. There are so many projects that are worthwhile, but as my mother-in-law says, "Women can do it all . . . but not all at the same time!"*
Words that best describe me: *Creative, caring, perfectionistic!*
I love to: *Read, sew, be a mommy*
I really don't care for: *People who are too busy to spend time with their kids — including their teenagers!*
If I could go anywhere in the world, it would be: *Chad, Africa — to see where my husband grew up*
In my lifetime I still want to: *Have more children*
It really bugs me when: *My plans don't work out. I'm very organized and have a terrible time improvising*
The thing that I love about youth ministry is: *The teens! It never fails to amaze me how eager they are to learn and be listened to*
My favorite place to spend time with God is: *Anywhere I won't be interrupted!*
If there is one thing that I would like to tell my colleagues, it would be: *Being a godly example is so much more important than programs! Teens today are starving for role models they can count on*

FOURTEEN

Cross-Gender Counseling
Guidelines for ministry effectiveness

by Steve Gerali, D.Phil. and Janice Gerali, RN

I had just finished speaking for a national youth conference and was boarding the plane to head back home to Chicago. I made my way to my seat and saw a man and woman already seated in the seats next to mine. As I pushed my briefcase into the overhead bin the woman said, "Hey, aren't you the guy that did the talk about counseling teenagers?" I affirmed that I was "the guy."

"We are volunteer workers with a youth group, and we need some advice about a counseling situation that our youth pastor is involved in," she said.

I sat down and buckled in. "Why do *you* need advice about a situation that *your* youth pastor is involved in?" I asked, confused.

"He shared the situation with us, and we think that he may have overstepped his boundaries in his advice and action to the student. We are planning to talk to him when we get home." My new friends proceeded to describe the following scenario.

The youth pastor had just been at this church for a year. He had come straight out of college and was doing an excellent job. He had built trust and rapport with the students to the extent that they felt free to disclose some of their personal issues. It seemed that one of the girls in the youth group had come to him with a problem. This girl was the daughter of a church board member and was dating a guy whose family was also involved in the leadership of this church. The girl needed advice about an issue and asked that the youth pastor not to disclose the information to her parents. The youth pastor agreed to keep things confidential. The student confessed that she and her boyfriend had been sexually active over the last few months. They both knew that it was not right for them to be sexually involved and had already set up boundaries to stop their sexual practices. The youth pastor was relieved to hear about their confession and new commitment. Again, the student affirmed that she didn't want her parents to know of the situation. She was afraid that it would crush and humiliate them. Again, the youth pastor affirmed confidence. At this point the girl felt free to disclose more of her situation.

Although they had stopped having sex, she was afraid that she was pregnant. She wasn't sure, but she knew that she was about two weeks late in her menstrual cycle, and she had always been very regular. If she knew that she was pregnant, she would have to tell her parents, but, if she wasn't, it would save two families and a church from a lot of pain.

This youth pastor was now faced with a dilemma. The only solution that this youth pastor could think of was to purchase a home pregnancy test for the student so that she could verify the pregnancy.

"We're having a difficult time with this and we think that he overstepped his boundaries," said the woman.

My response was that he in fact had overstepped his boundaries . . . a number of times. His actions could have a great, negative impact on the student, himself, and the church.

Many youth pastors have good intentions but little wisdom about cross-gender counseling. Often, this lack of wisdom puts them in situations over their heads. These seemingly small mistakes can mushroom into huge, complicated tragedies. Our society is litigation- and blame-happy. When people feel hurt or wronged, it is very easy to point to someone and cast blame to the extent that it becomes a legal battle. Many youth pastors have experienced this sting, and even if they didn't suffer legal retribution, they did suffer the loss of ministry through humiliation, lost trust, suspicion, and marred reputation.

It would be easy to say that we should never do any counseling but this would grossly compromise our ministries and be in violation of Christ's commands (Gal. 6:2). We could so restrict our ministry, to protect ourselves, that we diminish the value of the student. This type of ministry would be controlled by fear and that is not of God (2 Tim. 1:7).

THE NEED FOR CROSS-GENDER COUNSELING IN YOUTH MINISTRY

Youth workers will always give counsel to students. The population of adolescents is rapidly becoming known as an "at risk" population. More and more we are seeing students with great needs. They come into our ministries looking for safety, healing, support, and guidance. At one time, these were offered through parents and family. With the fragmenting and breakdown of the family, students must seek these in other settings. That means they will need to hear a masculine and feminine perspective of their situation. Cross-gender counseling is inevitable.

It would be strategic at this point to note that the tentativeness, concerns, and suspicions about cross-gender counseling do not only apply to male youth workers with female students but also for female youth workers with male students. While cross-gender counseling is inevitable in youth ministry, there are many principles that should govern it.

PRINCIPLE # 1: ESTABLISH CLEAR BOUNDARIES.

Boundaries establish safety for the student and the youth worker. A boundary defines the youth worker's and student's actions and responsibilities. Too often a youth worker's personal need-to-be-needed interferes in the establishment of clear boundaries. There are a number of boundaries that should define cross-gender counseling relationships.

Boundary # 1: You Are Not a Professional Counselor.
The first boundary is for the youth worker. Youth workers must realize that they are not professionally trained counselors. Many youth workers have minimal counseling training and attempt to tackle major psychological and emotional problems. This is comparable to a person with first-aid training trying to perform

open-heart surgery. At best, unless the youth worker has a professional counseling degree or credentials, he/she can only do interventional counseling until a professional counselor can become involved. A youth worker can do more to help a student if he/she builds a referral network of mental health professionals. Youth workers must know their limitations and see that they mobilize resources for a student in need.

Boundary # 2: There Is an Appropriate Time and Place for Cross-Gender Counseling.

The second boundary involves when and where a youth worker does counseling. I had a parent call me one day, stating that she was concerned because her daughter was talking to an adult male leader. The problem was not so much the leader as much as it was his wisdom of the counseling time and place. He seemed to get into these intense counseling sessions with the student late at night as he drove the student home. The sessions continued for a few hours while they sat in his car in the driveway of her house. This leader thought that he was exercising wisdom because the parents were aware that they were parked in the driveway.

Minor problems can easily escalate to crisis levels with adolescents. When it is late at night, a teen's problems can become more pronounced due to the fatigue of the day. This makes a student much more emotional and a youth worker more vulnerable. The student can formulate attachment issues and an unhealthy dependency on the youth worker. These issues can lead to fantasy and fabrication, on the part of the student, as to the true nature of the relationship. Verbal cues and advice can be misunderstood to convey more intimacy than is intended.

Youth workers should meet with opposite-gendered students when the student is at a relatively peak performance time. During the day, after school, or before a youth group meeting would be a wise choice. The youth worker should also set time parameters as to *how much* time should be spent in conversation about a problem. Most professional mental health workers spend 50–55 minutes with a client to assure a clarity of issues and maintain the boundary of the relationship.

Where a youth worker meets with a student is equally

important. This is often complicated because the youth worker must maintain the confidentiality of the student, yet not give the appearance of evil (1 Thes. 5:22) or fall vulnerable to Satan's attack (1 Peter 5:8). The best place for this to happen is in a public place, such as a restaurant. A youth worker should arrange to separately meet at a public place with the student and should leave separately from that public place. The problem that needs to be avoided when dealing with the time and location of the counseling session is *being alone,* one-to-one, with a member of the opposite gender. Traveling in a car to a site puts one in an equally vulnerable position as being secluded in a closed room. A restaurant creates an environment for a focused conversation, yet does not allow any room for things to be misunderstood. The noise of a restaurant or "white noise" creates a cocooning effect that helps the conversation stay on task. Being in a public place also eliminates any speculation as to the intimacy of the conversation.

If the time that a youth worker has with a student merits more of a closed, non-public setting, the youth worker should strategically plan this session. This type of counseling may be done in an office with open doors. The youth worker should make sure that someone else is aware of the meeting and present within sight of the room where the counseling occurs. Often it is best to make sure that the person present is the same gender as the student. The presence of another person makes the youth worker and the student accountable for their time together. It is not a bad practice for the youth worker to always be accountable for her/his counseling contacts whether it is in a private or public setting.

One youth worker made it a practice to meet her male students after school at a local fast food restaurant. She also would encourage them to bring one of their close friends to that session. Once, she arranged to meet with one student whom she thought might need to be in a clinically therapeutic setting. This youth worker tried to cover all of the bases. Her one mistake was that she allowed the student to control the accountability aspect. She asked him to bring a mutual friend along with him, someone with whom he felt comfortable sharing his problem. When the meeting time came, the friend never showed up. That youth worker learned that *she* needed to make the arrangement with the third party. If that person could not make the meeting, the youth worker could make other arrangements or reschedule the time with the student.

Boundary #3: Touch Must Be Guarded and Appropriate.

Appropriate touch is always a controversial issue with two very diverse poles. On one side of the continuum, we have those that are very free with touch or "tactile intimacy," arguing that Jesus was free with touch. Those who hold to this view say that Jesus took the children *in His arms* and blessed them (Mark 10:16). If we hold to an incarnational approach to student ministry, then we will be Christ's arms, hand, heart, etc. We demonstrate value for students when we touch them.

Recently, we walked into a store with our daughters. We were in a section where they displayed very expensive glassware. We grew increasingly nervous because one of our daughters wanted to handle the goods. I reminded her to read the "do not touch" signs and to refrain from touching. My daughter had demonstrated an instinctual human trait. That trait is evidenced in that when we see things that are valuable, we tend to want to touch them. Touch connotes value. When we touch students, we communicate value. In addition, when we understand the infinite value of our students, we want to demonstrate that by touch.

The other side of the continuum eliminates any touch whatsoever. Those who hold to this view say that touch is misunderstood in today's society. The argument could be made that society has a difficult time separating affectual touch and sexual touch. Someone who demonstrates a harmless, affectionate response can be mistaken to be overtly inappropriate. I have been made aware of ministries that have "no touch" rules. This would even exclude a friendly pat on the back or a warm touch on the shoulder. The consensus is that it is better to be safe and completely understood than to be sorry and jeopardize your ministry. Some may argue that this approach values one's ministry more than one's students, while those who hold to this view rightfully argue that they are being faithful stewards of what God has entrusted to them.

So then, where does a youth worker draw the line? What is appropriate and what is inappropriate? We must operate in the middle of this continuum, being wise in our touch. Appropriate touch can be regulated by the genuine regular practices of an individual and the setting in which touch is given.

Some youth ministries define the types of hugs (i.e., side-hugs, front-hugs, etc.) that are or are not allowed. The necessity of a "types of affection" definition could help some youth workers, but it may not eliminate the problem. For the most part, a youth worker who is naturally and genuinely affectionate with members of both sexes is less likely to be misunderstood than one who is restrained with his/her touch. People see the public displays of this worker's affection as a normal and authentic part of her/his response to students. Usually this is done in empathetic settings for a brief period of time. It is displayed regularly to both sexes, and it considers the receptivity of the student to touch.

Boundary # 4: Exercise Discretion on Subject Matter.

One youth worker recently shared a letter that he received from a student. He had been counseling her with reservation, so she opted to send him letters describing her problems. Although this youth worker thought that he had covered all the bases by limiting his contact with the student, he overlooked one important boundary. He did not define what was appropriate subject matter and the limits of her disclosure. The young girl's letters graphically described her relationally intimate problems and sexual exploits.

Often a student will sensationalize the problem by being overly graphic with her/his experiences. This can be arousing for the student (and the youth worker) and often is verbalized for "shock value." If boundaries are not defined, the student can fantasize about the subject matter, placing the youth worker in a voyeuristic role.

Youth workers who counsel in cross-gender contexts should limit the details of stories and determine if the subject matter is appropriate for that setting. If the subject matter is inappropriate for a cross-gender counseling context, the student should be referred to a counselor of the same sex. If a student is defensive about this, it may be an indication of a hidden agenda.

PRINCIPLE # 2: UNDERSTAND "CONFIDENTIALITY."

If we look back at the scenario opening the chapter, we will discover that the problem our youth pastor friend had began when he blindly agreed to confidentiality. Confidentiality has become a growing concern in youth ministry. We are encountering sexually and physically abused students in our ministry settings. The dilemma in which a youth worker is placed compounds when the safety of the student may be jeopardized by a parent. A youth pastor who discloses information to a parent could be acting irresponsibly. On the other hand, students have manipulated the system and youth professionals to gain attention or exact revenge against parents.

Confidentiality also becomes a concern in matters that are not abusive in nature. During the critical period of adolescence, a student must pull away from parents to form an autonomous identity. During this time a youth worker may become a significant adult confidant in that student's life. A youth worker must exercise wisdom in matters that he/she deems confidential. If that youth worker is too free to disclose information, she/he may compromise her/his ministry. Despite this, confidentiality must have definition and limitations.

A youth worker should immediately see "red flags" when a student starts a conversation by saying that he/she does not want anyone to know the content of what is about to be disclosed in the conversation. The most appropriate response to this would be for the youth worker to interrupt and not agree to keep things confidential until the subject matter and/or problem is disclosed.

The youth pastor at the beginning of the chapter was put into a trap. He had given his word and discovered, after the fact, that he was boxed in. Some youth workers are boxed in by giving their word that they will tell *nobody.* When this occurs, the youth worker cannot even consult a professional without betraying a trust. Professional consultation should regularly be sought in cross-gender counseling situations. A youth worker should be accountable to other staff members, advisors, and supervisors when involved in cross-gender counseling contexts. It is particularly wise to seek consultation from a member of the same sex as your student. This perspective can be valuable in understanding the dynamic of the situation as well as the content of the situation.

The law also has some limitations to confidentiality. Many states have "duty to warn" and "duty to protect" laws. This means that if a student reveals a situation that is clearly presenting a danger to an outside source, then the youth worker must inform either the authorities or the outside source. "Duty to warn" would include everything from a student who shares about a friend's suicidal ideation to a student's personal, homicidal ideation or vengeance threats.

"Duty to protect" involves the safety of the student. This would include verbalization and/or observation of abuse (physical or sexual); personal suicide ideation, or anything that jeopardizes the safety of the student (i.e. verbalization of eating disorders; drug and alcohol abuse; etc.). It is important that each youth worker becomes aware of the laws of his/her state regarding confidentiality. In addition, youth workers should devise a clear plan and criteria with their church regarding the contacting of the Department of Child and Family Services (DCFS) if there is suspected abuse. Contacts to DCFS can remain anonymous and DCFS will often coach a youth worker through proper procedures for individual situations. Most states with duty to warn/protect laws make it mandatory for people who work with minors (professionally or volunteer) to report abuse. This means that a youth worker can be held liable if he/she does not comply with the law.

PRINCIPLE # 3: HAVING A BALANCE BETWEEN "AUTHORITY" AND "RAPPORT": DEVELOPING A PARENTING STYLE THAT WILL KEEP THINGS SAFE.

Many youth workers find themselves in compromising positions because they haven't learned the balance between being an authority figure and being a friend to students. When this balance occurs, the youth worker will find himself/herself in a "parenting" type role.

Many compromise their authority by looking the other way when issues arise. Often, a youth worker will not confront the student. When disclosure occurs, the youth worker who compromises his/her authority will disregard boundaries for fear of lost intimacy. To this youth worker, creating an environment of acceptance seems to be threatened by boundaries. He/she may feel that the student will not disclose if the line of authority is maintained. The same youth worker may also have a difficult time seeing a harmonization between friendship and authority. If this imbalance occurs, the student will perceive the youth worker as a peer and not as a role model or authority. *If a student perceives a youth worker to be a peer, he/she will not perceive that youth worker to be a model.* A student's response is often different to a peer than it is to a role model or authority figure.

In a cross-gender counseling situation this imbalance can breed many unwarranted problems. Students may fantasize about the relationship, and a romantic "crush" could be the result of this imbalance. A student who is seeking emotional intimacy and bonding from an opposite-sex counselor can misunderstand or fantasize the dynamic of the relationship.

One youth worker described her "fatal attraction" incident. She felt that a male student whom she was counseling was developing an unhealthy attraction to her. This relationship soon became a sure thing in the mind of the student, and he responded with flowers, notes, inappropriate phone calls, and even stalked her in a non-hostile manner. This youth worker tried to rectify the situation by confronting the student and clarifying the relationship. It ended up appearing to be an ugly "break-up" to the student and many onlookers. This youth worker could have avoided a lot of trouble if the line of authority (boundaries) and rapport (support) were balanced. She had made some mistakes by allowing students to call at all hours of the day, allowing students to speak inappropriately in her presence, and not maintaining relationships with a network of friends her own age, among other things. All of these factors contributed to the imbalance. Students must view a youth worker on the same strata as parents or quality caregivers.

PRINCIPLE # 4: INVOLVE THE STUDENT WITH A SAME-GENDER COUNSELOR WHENEVER POSSIBLE.

This principle seems too obvious to mention, but it is the most overlooked principle. There are many issues that complicate follow-through on this point.

The foremost issue to muddy these waters is a trust issue. When a student is emotionally vulnerable to a youth worker, it is hard to pass off that student because it plays the heartstrings of the youth worker. Vulnerability is, in fact, a bonding phenomenon. Youth workers, who initially experience this phenomenon, may not trust that the student will understand the referral, perceiving that the youth worker's actions are cold and heartless. A good caregiver will take time to be understood and verbalize his/her limitations which may interfere with the quality of care given to the student.

This trust issue also manifests itself in that a youth worker may feel there are no qualified same-gendered counselors who will understand this student's problem. The youth worker who feels this often does not refer the student to someone else because he/she has strong desires to be involved in the counseling process, for one reason or another. This is another evidence of the need-to-be-needed syndrome that was mentioned earlier. Same-gender counselors with relational skills and who have a balanced rapport/authority relationship with students should be entrusted with same-gender counseling roles.

I was made aware of a situation by a youth pastor who said that he was all his youth group had. He meant that literally. He had a small youth ministry with about 10 students involved. He had been trying to recruit a volunteer female staff person but had not successfully completed the task. In the meantime he found himself in a few cross-gender counseling situations and didn't know how to respond. My suggestion was that he involve any significant woman from his life (such as a wife, female friend, committee member, secretary, etc.) in that counseling situation. He should clearly define the boundaries for the student and make sure the student knows this person is there for her input and perceptions. When a situation like this arises, the youth worker must let the student know in advance that there will be another person present at the meeting. He and his partner must assure confidentiality (within the previously discussed limits) to the student.

When a joint counseling situation is engaged, the opposite-gendered counselor must allow the same-gendered counselor to lead the session as much as possible. The opposite-gendered counselor plays a supportive role. This may be hard for some who feel the need to be controlling. If the control issue can be overcome, this will be the most effective kind of cross-gender counseling.

DON'T MINISTER ALONE

Effective counseling is an important part of today's youth ministries. By using these guidelines it is our hope that you can meet the needs of your students more effectively. As stated in previous chapters, we were never meant to minister alone. By developing a network of caring professionals to work alongside your ministry, your students will get the quality care they deserve.

BARRIER BREAKERS

1. Have you ever found yourself in difficult cross-gender counseling situations?

2. After reading this chapter, what would you do differently?

3. Do you have counselors whom you can call for advice or for student referrals? If not, what steps can you take to be better prepared for the future?

4. In talking about the balance between authority and rapport, where do you find yourself? Do you need to make some adjustments in order to minister more effectively?

Author

Name: *Steve Gerali*

Occupation: *Professor of Youth Ministry and Department Chair at Judson College and Psychotherapist*

Birthplace: *Chicago*

The last movie that significantly impacted me was: Schlinder's List

The style that best reflects me is: *Eclectic*

Favorite childhood memory: *Disneyland*

A good book that I would recommend is: Loving God *by Charles Colson*

I've never been able to: *Sky-dive*

Nobody knows I'm: *Annoyed by having to talk on the telephone*

If I could do it over: *I'd have gone to medical school*

I'm working on: *A new book*

Word that best describes me: *Ambitious*

I love to: *Listen*

If I could go anywhere in the world, it would be: *Europe*

In my lifetime I still want to: *Be part of a presidential cabinet*

It really bugs me when: *People are selfish*

My favorite place to spend time with God is: *In my car while I'm driving*

One of my passions is to: *Help heal hurting adolescents*

If there is one thing that I would like to tell my colleagues, it would be: *God alone*

Name: *Janice Gerali*
Occupation: *Registered nurse*
Birthplace: *Chicago*
Children: *Andrea (10) and Alison (8)*
Favorite childhood memory: *Camping on the beach*
A good book that I would recommend is: *The Zion Covenant series by Bodie Thoene*
My favorie food is: *Pizza*
I've never been able to: *Scuba-dive*
If I could do it over: *I'd be a nurse anesthetist*
In my lifetime I still want to: *Go back to school*
Word that best describes me: *Fun-loving*
I love to: *Snow ski*
If I could go anywhere in the world, it would be: *Australia*
One of my passions is: *My children*
If there is one thing that I would like to tell my colleagues, it would be: *My interest in people, not things*

FIFTEEN

Finishing Well
Equipped for the journey

by Lynn Ziegenfuss

I have fought the good fight, I have finished the race, I have kept the faith (2 Timothy 4:7, NRSV).

When I started working full-time in youth ministry, the farthest thing from my mind was finishing well. Why would anyone want to discuss finishing when she is just beginning? Eighteen years later, after watching too many people leave youth ministry tired, bitter or, worse yet, totally broken, I've discovered the value of continually considering this issue throughout my ministry. Taking steps now to finish well in ministry will greatly influence our attitudes and choices as the weeks and months turn into years of working with young people. Whatever your experience, it is time to consider how well you'll finish.

What do I mean by finishing well? I remember attending my father's retirement dinner. Several people spoke of his accomplishments, his influence in their lives and, after 33 years, the legacy he was leaving behind as a coach and professor at San Diego State University. My father *finished* well. The example of completing a chapter in our life is the primary aspect of what I mean by finishing. However, the completion of chapters in our lives contributes to how we finish our life in the ultimate sense. Thus, there will be times in this discussion when the phrase, "finishing well," can be applied both to our ministry and to our entire life.

The second word of the phrase, *well,* also has a double meaning. *Wellness* is really two sides of one coin. *Webster's* definition of *well* is "to be in good health." We can assume that this definition has implications for ministry that include our emotional health, spiritual health, and our physical health. The challenge for us in ministry is to learn how to take care of ourselves. We must seek to be healthy and whole so we don't burn out, but end *well*. There's another definition of the word, *well*. It means, "to end in a proper and right manner." In a spiritual sense, wellness means to honor God with our life, and not to discredit the Gospel. The Apostle Paul was very concerned about finishing well. In Acts 20:24, he writes, "But I do not count my life of any value to myself, if only I may finish my course and the ministry that I received from the Lord Jesus, to testify to the good news of God's grace" (NRSV).

In 1 Corinthians 9:24-27, we read:

> "Do you not know that in a race the runners all compete, but only one receives the prize. Run in such a way that you may win it. Athletes exercise self-control in all things; they do it to receive a perishable wreath; but we an imperishable one. So I do not run aimlessly, nor do I box as though beating the air; but I punish my body and enslave it, so that after proclaiming to others I myself should not be disqualified" (NRSV).

Paul, indeed, was concerned about finishing well. In chapter 9 of 1 Corinthians, Paul is talking about his ministry as an apostle. These verses illustrate the work and effort involved in running as a leader in this race, called life, and in completing the task in a "proper and right manner."

Today's decisions, choices, and disciplines, or lack of them, in our lives all have an impact on how we complete our ministry. We need to talk about finishing because we have an enemy who does not want us to finish well. We read in 1 Peter 5:8, "Discipline yourselves, keep alert. Like a roaring lion your adversary the devil prowls around, looking for someone to devour" (NRSV). The enemy is especially looking for leaders to discredit. In the last ten years of my ministry I've seen how the enemy has discredited people I care about because of the choices they have made. I've worked under three different leaders, two of whom were disqualified from ministry because of their choices. A year ago, my pastor of eleven years, a man with a twenty-eight-year career, was disqualified from ministry because of his choices.

Unfortunately, my experiences are not the exception. Haven't we all known or heard stories of someone in ministry who did not finish well?

The struggle to finish well is not just a twentieth-century phenomenon. We need only look to the Old Testament to see other examples. Israel's first king, Saul, had a miserable ending. King David took a major detour in his life and leadership because of his unbridled passion. King Solomon was the wisest man that ever lived. Though he started out very well, let's remember how he ended. Solomon had 700 wives and 300 concubines. "For when Solomon was old, his wives turned away his heart after other gods; and his heart was not true to the LORD his God" (1 Kings 11:4, NRSV). As a result of Solomon's actions, God's people, the Israelites, were divided. This created a ripple effect that impacts us even today. It can be discouraging when we read these accounts, and the prevailing question then becomes, is it possible for anyone to finish well?

YES! God's grace, acknowledging our need for help, and making healthy, deliberate, disciplined choices is how believers can finish well. I want to focus on four on-going CHOICES I believe we must start making NOW in order to finish well in ministry and in life.

EMBRACE OUR WOUNDEDNESS RATHER THAN DENY IT

We all have wounds. Unfulfilled dreams, illness, shame, and disappointments that all contribute to our experience of being broken. God can use our brokenness if we are willing to embrace it. We need to recognize pain as part of our life. God uses our pain to build our character. Haven't you experienced a connection with others when they share a broken place in their lives, making themselves vulnerable? Sometimes when I speak to a group, I share my struggle of being single. I'm always amazed at the response of the audience. Invariably, they feel connected to me, not because of any principle or thought I have shared, but because I took the risk of sharing my pain. We are all comforted to know that other people are broken and that we are not alone.

Our broken places unite us.

Yet if we deny our brokenness, those wounds will surface and get met in very unhealthy ways. Have you ever played with a beach ball or volleyball in water? When you try to hold a ball under water, eventually it pops up. You wrestle to hold the ball under the water's surface, yet you can't hold it down forever. It eventually pops up. The harder you try to shove it down, the bigger the eruption. This is exactly what can happen with our wounds. Somewhere, somehow when we try to stuff or deny our pain below the surface, it pops out. Unhealthy needs will always find a way to get met. Either we project our wounds onto other people or we inappropriately get "tied up" with young people in our ministry in a way that we shouldn't. What is even worse, as in the case of one of my former colleagues, we might cross over a clear boundary and get involved in a sexual relationship to meet a need to be close to somebody — an act that is devastating to all involved!

What is threatening about denying our woundedness is that it gives a foothold for Satan. Denial becomes our Achilles heal, and the evil one knows it. Satan is the master of lies and would like to convince us to forget our pain and not deal with it. Satan systematically seeks to destroy us with this strategy. Being single is an Achilles heel for me. It's certainly not what I planned for my life. I come from a close family and always envisioned that I'd have a big family of my own. My not being married is a painful part of my life, so I want to run from it. My tendency is to throw myself into work so I don't have to live in that painful place. When I try to submerge the pain, I find myself thinking destructive thoughts. I ask myself, *What's wrong with me? Have I done something wrong?* This destructive behavior can lead to depression, withdrawing in relationships, and a lack of closeness to God. These questions and doubts give a foothold to Satan. The evil one will do anything to fight against our finishing well!

We all have wounded places and we must embrace them. In his book *Honest to God?* Bill Hybels says,

> There is healing power in sharing our inner hurts with someone else. There's a release, a catharsis, that makes the burden seem lighter. Sometimes just having someone affirm the legitimacy of our pain eases it a little. There's also the obvious benefit of receiving guidance

from those with whom we share. Overwhelming issues suddenly become manageable when a friend offers an insight or suggests a course of action we hadn't thought of.[1]

We must own our pain and face our wounds, so we can do something about them. If we don't confront them, I am convinced they will get in the way of having a healthy long-term ministry. Our first choice, therefore, must be to embrace our woundedness rather than deny it.

CHOOSE TRANSPARENCY OVER AN IMAGE

When we hide our pain, then we have to create an image by which to live because we are afraid to be real. Unfortunately, many people in ministry live their lives based on image. Their leadership is focused on what they think other people want from them or how they should be. Energy is spent on selling the image, second guessing others, and covering up who they really are. A myth in our culture tells us that we should have it all together if we are in leadership. We fall prey to the belief that if we have some weakness, we can't be used as leaders.

My first year in full-time ministry was one of the most difficult times in my life. During that time I was always tired from working *long* hours week after week. When I wasn't working, I felt guilty. I spent little time with the Lord. I was struggling financially. Yet the biggest problem was, no one knew I was dying inside. I walked into the office every day and acted as if everything was fine. I portrayed an image. Since that time I have met with *many* youth workers who are caught in that similar place of living out an image. Nobody really knows them. I'm thankful for the lessons and freedom that I've carried from those early experiences, such as, learning and admitting my limits (I can't work sixty hours week after week), and I'm not indispensable!

The bottom line is that when you create an image, you are living dishonestly. You are living dishonestly with God, with yourself, with your coworkers, and with the kids with whom you minister. The lie you tell yourself is, "*I* can handle it, *I'm* doing fine." Yet the question we must ask is, where is Jesus in all this? Christ is supposed to be the Lord of our life and ministry. Are you out to prove that you can do this thing called full-time youth ministry on your own? It's only when you can admit "who you really are" and that you may not "have it all together" that transparency begins. We must start first by telling God, and then we must tell at least one other person. Transparency takes courage and is a moment-by-moment choice. Scripture tells us, "for whenever I am weak, then I am strong" (2 Corinthians 12:10, NRSV). There is power when we allow the Lord to work through our weaknesses, and, many times, God uses our greatest weaknesses as incredible tools for Him.

Creating an image is the greatest disservice we can do to the kids to whom we minister. We give them the impression that to be a Christian means we are perfect. Our deception sets up our young followers to fail. They can feel defeated and ultimately conclude that Christianity isn't for them, or that they're not good enough.

Do you pretend to have it together? Do you have an approach to life to "buck up and press on"? This is not helpful to people who are hurting. Struggling people feel as if they have to live up to an image to be accepted. In my opinion that is why there are many frustrated and powerless Christians.

A coworker of mine was seeking transparency instead of image. While attending a twelve-step program, he experienced more authentic caring and concern than he had ever experienced in the church. With people who had hit rock bottom, he learned to be transparent. It's a sad commentary when the church does not invite us to be honest about our life struggles.

Transparency and honesty will help you embrace your woundedness. You'll be more open to hear from God about the ways you need to grow and where God wants to lead you. When working so hard at the image thing, it is hard for us to hear the Lord because we spend all of our energy trying to be someone we are not.

Transparency and honesty also make us more approachable to the people to whom we minister. In *What Return Can I Make*, M. Scott Peck says,

Mature Christians are called to the disarmament movement. If Jesus taught us anything, He taught us that the way to salvation lies though vulnerability. He opened himself to the poor, the prostitutes, the lepers, the cripples, the foreigners, the outcasts, the untouchables. . . . What happens when one person says to another: "I'm confused, I'm feeling lost and lonely, will you help me?" The effect of such vulnerability is almost invariably disarming. . . . But what happens if we try to maintain a macho image of having it all together, of being the top dog, when we gird ourselves about with our psychological defenses? We become inapproachable, and our neighbors gird themselves in their defenses, and our human relationships become no more meaningful or productive than two empty tanks bumping together in the night.[2]

If we pretend to have it all together, will we be approachable to those who are broken? Our portrayal may make others feel judged, and they may not share their real selves. For the sake of our ministry, we must embrace our woundedness. For the health and growth of our ministry, we must choose transparency.

COMMUNITY AND NOT ISOLATION

When we deny our woundedness and put up an image, then the only way to exist is in isolation . . . so we don't get found out. Bad choices, secret sins, and double lives usually occur from isolation. Habits and/or addictions, such as substance abuse or eating disorders, start to control people who are running from pain, stuck in an image and alone in their thinking. They live with the distorted reality that no one can understand their struggle.

Isolation is a great strategy of Satan in the life of a leader. Leaders can be lonely people because they back themselves into a corner. Let me clarify that I'm not talking about a leader who feels alone because of her or his role of making decisions and motivating people to follow a vision. I'm talking about leaders who are isolated because they try to live behind the mask of perfection. In reality they have weaknesses, but are too afraid to admit them. Image and appearance can pave the road to living a hidden life, filled with destructive behavior.

People really want their leaders to be vulnerable. When I took the risk of admitting that I was in a spiritual desert and feeling distant from God, I found that people were drawn to my honesty and in turn wanted to share their own struggles. Trust, safety, and closeness result from this type of openness. A leader's honesty models and gives permission for others to be honest. True community cannot be known where there is not honesty. Haven't you experienced a time when a pastor or speaker shares from his or her heart about a personal struggle? Transparency draws people together instead of encouraging them to be alone in their pain.

The good news is that God has called us into community. He has called us to be a family. We all need to come and kneel before the Cross. We are sinners saved by grace who stand on the same ground. Whatever is your circumstance in life: married, single, rich, poor, pretty, ugly, fat, skinny, black, white, it doesn't matter. Ours is a God who calls us into a relationship with Him and with others.

Let's examine a few dimensions of what I mean by choosing community. Community can happen in the context of a sole confidant or a small group. Accountability and authenticity are two pillars which build community. Time and time again we read or hear about Christian leaders who have fallen because they had no accountability. They chose isolation!

As a youth worker and Christian leader, you need at least one person in your life *and* a small group with whom you can be totally honest. We need someone who will ask the hard questions, questions that we may not *want* to hear, but we *need* to hear. Those people are gifts to our life. Proverbs 27:6 says, "Faithful are the wounds of a friend, but deceitful are the kisses of an enemy" (NASB). We need friends who are willing to tell us the truth. Community allows us to have accountability and, on the other side, gives us the opportunity to experience grace from others as we admit our weaknesses and failures. Sometimes it's really hard to sense God's grace and forgiveness. But when it's fleshed out by your sisters and brothers, they, at those points, represent Jesus. I love the way Henri Nouwen explains this choice in *The Wounded Healer:*

A shared pain is no longer paralyzing but mobilizing, when understood as a way to liberation. When we become aware that we do not have to escape our pains, but that we can mobilize them into a common search for life, those very pains are transformed from expressions of despair into signs of hope. . . . Christian community is therefore a healing community not because wounds are cured and pains are alleviated, but because wounds and pains become openings or occasions for a new vision. Mutual confession then becomes a mutual deepening of hope, and sharing weakness becomes a reminder to one and all of the coming strength. . . . Community arises where the sharing of pain takes place, not a stifling form of self-complaint, but as a recognition of God's saving promises.[5]

If you do not have a small group; if you don't have someone in your life with whom you can be very, very honest, in my mind, it's the number one priority you need to address in your life.

The Scriptures tell the story of God's family, His chosen people. We see, time and again, examples of God working with a group of people, not just individuals. Rarely does God call us out alone without the accountability and support of the body. We live in a country where a fundamental value is to be independent, to be an individual. Independence isn't bad in and of itself. For the Christian, however, independence creates a tension because we have also chosen to follow Jesus Christ who calls us to submission. In order to have Jesus Christ be the Lord of our life, we must choose not to act independently from Him. The Scriptures command and a healthy Christian community requires that we "submit one to another" (Eph. 5:21) and "confess your sins to each other" (James 5:16). Integrating independence and submission is a struggle, especially in the American culture. The discipline, however, is well worth the effort as community is vital to finishing well.

CHOOSE AN ADVENTURESOME SPIRITUAL JOURNEY

Too many in ministry have an approach to God which suggests, "see how hard I'm working for You, God?" If your reason for being in ministry is an attempt to earn God's love, I have good news for you! There is **nothing** you can do to make God love you more or cause God to love you less than He does at this very minute. He loves you perfectly. Serving in ministry does not earn brownie points in God's eyes. In fact, one reason you may be called into youth ministry is because it is where God can best mold **your** character. Your call to youth ministry is more about **you** than what you do for Him. We are given a wonderful privilege by God who allows us to be involved in the transformation of young peoples' lives. Isn't it great to watch kids lives change? It's thrilling!

How do we choose an adventuresome spiritual journey? We choose to nurture intimacy with Jesus Christ. A relationship with Jesus calls us on a journey. There are going to be bumpy times, times when things are really dry, times when you feel distant from God and others. Even in those times we are still on the journey. So then, how do we make it adventuresome? Creativity, variety, and newness all contribute to a dynamic journey, filled with adventure. Any long-term relationship, such as marriage, requires work and investment. My parents have been married fifty-four years and, believe me, over the years they have had some very bumpy roads. But one of the things as I was growing up that I always saw my parents do was have a lot of variety in their lives. They traveled, had lots of friends, went camping, did things with and without their kids. The same is true in getting to know Jesus.

My concern is that often in the evangelical church we have two ways of knowing God — prayer and Bible Study. We call it quiet time. Those things are very important. However, God is a big God. There are lots of ways to know Him. Though I think Bible study and prayer are fundamental and primary, I would like to challenge your thinking in discovering other ways to nurture an intimate relationship with Him.

About twelve years ago I went on a silent retreat with my church for an entire weekend to a retreat center run by Benedictine monks. There were over thirty people. I'll never forget how nervous I was the first evening. Hours of silence with other people around was a strange, but curious, adventure. I loved it! Removing the external noises helped me to create a space and listen to God's "still small voice" like never before. What an adventure I had with God and have had, ever since, as I've continued the discipline of silence. If you are curious, I highly recommend the adventure. Start with a few hours at a park, in the mountains, or at a retreat center. Invite a few friends or, better yet, your small group!

Journaling is another way to get to know God. Use your journal to have conversations. Literally ask God a question and wait to see how He might answer. Then journal that response. Or recall or describe an experience in your life. As you write, see what comes from that journaling. Ask yourself some questions like, "How have I changed?" or "What did I learn about myself in this experience?" That's a discipline. Some people don't like to put pen and paper together. Personally, I can best journal when I'm alone in a quiet place, but not at home — too many distractions. If I'm really stuck or overwhelmed in some feelings or have a big decision to make, journaling seems to be very helpful.

There are many other ways or disciplines you can practice to keep your walk with Jesus fresh and not routine. Be bold and venture out — I dare you!

What about the people who have taken detours that were not what God intended? The ones that didn't finish well in terms of a chapter in their life. They may have made choices that disqualified them from returning to a particular ministry, but, because of God's grace, they can still finish well in terms of their Christian life. He wants all of His children to finish well. He brings healing. He is our hope. He doesn't abandon us when we mess up. That's the good news! However, this does not prevent the individual from experiencing the consequences of poor choices. He or she may not be able to go back to a ministry to take back the pain caused to others. Worse yet, no one can change the shaken faith of others, caused by a fallen, once respected leader. God has to do that work. Hopefully, though, in the midst of brokenness and rebuilding one's Christian life, the devastation and shame won't hinder the hurting leader from turning back to God. He is there as the Savior and Immanuel to forgive our sins and to be with us to heal our hearts. I would hope that these individuals could learn to make the right choices in their lives that allow them to become the person that God intended.

As you have prayed through the many challenges in this

book, I hope that God gives you many enriching years as a woman or man in youth ministry. I pray that God will give you the courage to choose to embrace your wounds, to be transparent, to be in community, and to have a spiritual journey full of new adventures in knowing Him, so that, when all is said and done, you can say to the Father, as Jesus did in John 17:4, "I glorified you on earth by finishing the work that you gave me to do" (NRSV).

BARRIER BREAKERS

1. How will you know if you've finished well in youth ministry?

2. Are there wounds in your life that you have tried to deny? If so, how can you face your woundedness and use it for good in your life?

3. Are there people in your life with whom you can be transparent?

4. What are you doing to continue growing on your spiritual journey?

Author

Name: *Lynn Ziegenfuss*

Occupation: *Training Director, YFC/USA*
Current home: *Denver, Colorado*
My favorite food is: *Cookies*
Nobody knows: *I love doing jigsaw puzzles*
If I were a famous painter, I'd paint: *Yosemite Valley and Half Dome*
I'm working on: *The inside of my house. It takes a loooong time and lots of money, which is why it takes a loooong time*
If I weren't in youth ministry, I'd be: *A teacher*
Words that best describe me: *Loyal, fun, straightforword*
I love to: *Play games with friends (cards, board games, any kind) and go to the movies*
If I could go anywhere in the world, it would be: *Back to Israel with a group of close friends*
In my life time I still want to: *Go to every premiere sports event (World Series, Super Bowl, Indy 500, etc.)*
My favorite pet is: *A cuddly dog*
It really bugs me when: *People honk their horn when a light has just turned green*
The thing that I love about youth ministry is: *Seeing kids' lives change and working with committed, creative, and fun people!*
One of my passions is to: *Visit every continent*
I've learned that: *Life really doesn't ever get easy*
If there is one thing that I would like to tell my colleagues, it would be: *To love one another by believing the best and encouraging each other*
I would like to be remembered for: *Being a creative and fun friend, having integrity, making a difference, and being a good and faithful servant in the kingdom of God*

Notes

Introduction

1. Mark Senter, *The Coming Revolution in Youth Ministry* (Wheaton, Illinois: Victor Books, 1992), 143.

Chapter 1: Beyond Kitchens and Kool-Aid

1. Aristotle, "The Difference between Men and Women," *History of Ideas on Women: A Sourcebook*, ed. Rosemary Agonito (New York: Perigee, 1977), 46.

2. Thomas Aquinas, *Summa Theologica*, part 1, question 92: "The Production of the Woman," *Women and Religion*, ed. Elizabeth Clark and Herbert Richardson (San Francisco: Harper Collins Publishers, 1977), 87.

3. Immanuel Kant, "The Interrelations of the Two Sexes," *History of Ideas on Women: A Sourcebook*, ed. Rosemary Agonito (New York: Perigee, 1977), 142.

4. David L. Smith, *A Handbook of Contemporary Theology* (Wheaton, Illinois: BridgePoint, 1992), 241.

5. Ruth A. Tucker, *Woman in the Maze* (Downers Grove, Illinois: InterVarsity Press, 1992), 90.

6. Mardi Keyes, "Are Christianity and Feminism Compatible?" L'Abri Conference Speech (March 1993), 6.

7. James Hurley, *Man and Woman in Biblical Perspective* (Grand Rapids, Michigan: Zondervan, 1981), 216.

8. Keyes, "Are Christianity and Feminism Compatible?" 7.

9. Mary Hayter, *The New Eve in Christ: The Use and Abuse of the Bible in the Debate about Women in Christ* (Grand Rapids, Michigan: Eerdmans, 1987), 101.

10. Tertullian, *On Apparel of Women* 2:1 in *Ante-Nicene Fathers*, vol. 4, ed. Alexander Roberts and James Donaldson (New York: Scribner's, 1925), 18.

11. Tucker, *Woman in the Maze*, 45.

12. Mary Stewart Van Leeuwen, *Grace and Gender* (Downers

Grove, Illinois: InterVarsity Press, 1990), 47.

13. Tucker, *Woman in the Maze,* 51.

14. Keyes, "Are Christianity and Feminism Compatible?" 11–12.

15. Faith Martin, *Call Me Blessed: The Emerging Christian Woman* (Grand Rapids, Michigan: Eerdmans, 1988), 34.

16. Ibid., 128.

17. Tucker, *Woman in the Maze,* 65–69.

18. Dorothy Sayers, *Are Women Human?* (Grand Rapids, Michigan: Eerdmans, 1988), 47.

19. Robert M. Mulholland, " The Role of Women in the Church," Women in Ministry class lecture at Asbury Theological Seminary (Spring 1994), 1–3.

20. Ibid., 5.

21. Keyes, "Are Christianity and Feminism Compatible?" 4–6.

22. Ibid., 9.

23. Tucker, *Woman in the Maze,* 114.

24. Aida Besancon Spencer, *Beyond the Curse: Women Called to Ministry* (Nashville, Tennessee: Thomas Nelson, 1985), 75.

25. Richard Kroeger and Catherine Clark, "May Women Teach?" *Christians for Biblical Equality* newsletter reprint, 1–4.

26. Keyes, "Are Christianity and Feminism Compatible?" 11–12.

27. Ibid., 13.

28. Mulholland, "The Role of Women in the Church," 5.

29. Keyes, "Are Christianity and Feminism Compatible?" 11–12.

30. Fred D. Layman, "Male Headship in Paul's Thought" *Wesleyan Theological Journal,* vol. 15, no. 1 (Spring 1980), 52.

31. Tucker, *Woman in the Maze,* 147.

32. Ibid., 143–190.

Chapter 2: Maximizing Our Differences

1. Ruth Herrman Siress, *Working Woman's Communications Survival Guide* (New Jersey: Prentice Hall, 1994), 184–85.

2. Deborah Tannen, *You Just Don't Understand: Men and Women in Conversation* (New York: Ballantine Books, 1990), 89–90.

3. Ken Davis, Interview with author, 8 August 1994.

4. Ibid.

5. Lynn Ziegenfuss, Interview with author, "Power behind the Podium,"*Journey* 16, August 1995, 2–3.

6. Davis interview, 8 August 1994.

7. Ibid.

8. Ibid.

9. Tannen, *You Just Don't Understand,* 127–29.

10. Ibid., 236–37.

11. Ibid., 237.

12. Ibid., 148.

13. Ibid., 153–54.

14. Ibid., 236.

15. Ibid., 77.

16. Ibid., 183.

Chapter Three: Ministry Would Be Great If It Weren't for the People

1. Dietrich Bonhoeffer, *Life Together* (San Francisco: Harper, 1976), 26–27.

2. Ibid.

3. Bob Phillips, *The Delicate Art of Dancing with Porcupines: Learning to Appreciate the Finer Points of Others* (Ventura, California: Regal, 1989), 54–55.

Chapter Four: Dynamic Duos

1. After working at the same church, San Diego First Assembly of God for four years, we now serve as youth workers at different churches in San Diego. However, we continue to practice the principles of being a dynamic duo through citywide and regional event planning and joint ministry projects.

Chapter Seven: Barriers along the Way

1. Adapted from *Journey* (Spring 1994).

2. Winston A. Johnson, "Gender, Society, and Church," *Gender Matters: Women's Studies for the Christian Community,* ed. J.S. Hagem (Grand Rapids, Michigan: Academie/Zondervan, 1990), 24.

Chapter Eight: You're Not Alone

1. John F. Gillespie, "To Network—or Not Work," *Financial Executive,* vol. 9, no. 4 (July–August 1993), 48.

2. Dan Kempel, *Networking in the Music Business* (Cincinnati, Ohio: Writer's Digest Books, 1993), 2.

3. Mary Scott Welch, *Networking, the Great New Way for Women to Get Ahead* (New York: Harcourt Brace Jovanovich, 1980), 15.

Chapter Nine: What Men Can Do to Help

1. Andrew M. Greeley, *When Life Hurts* (New York: Doubleday & Co., Inc., 1988).

Chapter Thirteen: When Bandages Aren't Enough

1. Josh McDowell, *The Myths of Sex Education* (San Bernardino, California: Here's Life Publishers, 1990), 159.

2. Dr. Joe S. McIlhaney, Jr., *Sexuality and Sexually Transmitted Diseases* (Grand Rapids, Michigan: Baker Book House, 1990), 148.

3. Josh McDowell, *The Myths of Sex Education,* 10.

4. C. Bohmer, and A. Parrot, *Sexual Assault on Campus—The Problem and the Solution* (New York: Lexington Books, 1993), 1.

Chapter Fifteen: Finishing Well

1. Bill Hybels, *Honest to God?* (Grand Rapids, Michigan: Zondervan, 1990), 103.

2. M. Scott Peck, *What Return Can I Make?* (New York: Simon and Schuster, 1985), 151–52.

3. Henri Nouwen, *The Wounded Healer* (New York: Doubleday, 1979), 93–94.

Appendix
Resources for Effective Ministry

Compiled by Jean Tippit

The following is a list of various resources a youth minister may find. The list is divided into four main groups: (1) training organizations, (2) periodicals, (3) crisis resources, and (4) program resources. This list is not comprehensive and does not contain denominational headquarters and publishers. For more resources a youth minister could check out the local Christian bookstores, other youth ministers, and their denominational headquarters.

TRAINING ORGANIZATIONS

These organizations each offer various types of training, designed to help equip the youth workers of today.

Group Publishing
1-800-447-1070
Group offers many training opportunities through one-day events held in major U. S. cities and their annual "Kidstitute: the Ministry Conference to Children, Youth and Families."

National Network of Youth Ministry
1-619-951-1111
Network is a nondenominational, membership organization that links youth workers together for encouragement, spiritual growth, and resource sharing for the purpose of being more effective in youth ministry. In addition, they sponsor training events that facilitate their vision as well as national projects such as, "See You at the Pole."

National Institute of Youth Ministry
1-714-498-4418
NIYM is committed to training youth ministers and offers a large range of training opportunities. These opportunities include one- to two-day intensive training seminars which can be done at your local church or city, week-long training institutes, and advance training for those wishing to train others.

Journey Publications
P.O. Box 594
Lincolnshire, IL 60069
Journey is a membership organization supporting the leadership development of volunteer and professional women in youth ministry. Journey's membership includes a speaker bureau, job opportunity listing, and training newsletters. Journey also offers national and regional conference training events.

Youth Specialties
1-800-776-8008
Youth Specialties sponsors the National Youth Workers Convention. The conventions provide youth workers the opportunity to gain valuable training to use in their work with teens, resources, a look at current Christian entertainment, and an opportunity to network with other youth ministers across the nation. Youth Specialties also offers one-day resource seminars in major cities throughout the year. These one-day seminars are led by veterans of youth ministry and offer a great deal of information about ministry to students.

PROGRAM MATERIALS

The companies listed below each carry a variety of different material including Sunday School curriculum, Bible study materials, devotionals, how-to books, and much more.

David C. Cook
1-800-323-7543
4005 Lee Vance Dr.
Colorado Springs, CO 80918

Gospel Light
1-800-4-GOSPEL
P. O. Box 3875
Ventura, California 93006-9891

Group
1-800-447-1070
P. O. Box 485
Loveland, Colorado 80539

National Institute of Youth Ministry
1-714-498-4418
P. O. Box 4374
San Clemente, California 92674

Scripture Press
1-800-323-9409
1825 College Avenue
Wheaton, Illinois 60187

Youth Specialties
1-800-776-8008
1224 Greenfield Drive
El Cajon, California 92021

PERIODICALS

The following periodicals are just a few of the magazines available to youth workers.

Called Together Ministries
20820 Avis Avenue
Torrance, CA 90503
1-310-793-9747
CTM ministers to pastor's wives and women in ministry. This group offers an extensive mail-order resource catalog, a "Listening Line" for telephone peer counseling, referral services, a free newsletter, retreats, and seminars.

Campus Life
1-800-678-6083
This magazine is designed for the Christian high school or college student. It offers helps in all areas of the student life and makes a great gift idea for special events.

Contemporary Christian Music (CCM)
P.O. Box 555
Boulder, Colorado 80321-5996
For up-to-the-minute information on the contemporary Christian music scene, this magazine is a must have. It offers insight into what is hot and what is not, as well as the inside scoop on many of today's Christian artists.

Group and Jr. High Ministry Magazines
1-800-447-1070
These two magazines are filled with resource listings, programming ideas, helpful articles both for personal and professional use, and information on current news and fads.

Journey Publications
P.O. Box 594
Lincolnshire, IL 60069
Journey addresses the unique needs of women in youth ministry as well as highlighting specialized needs for girls' ministry and effective team ministry.

Youthworker Journal
1-800-769-7624
The *Journal* is a great resource for the youthworker who wants to understand teens, parents, the church, and other related aspects of ministry. Articles published in the *Journal* come from youth ministers, pastors, and Christian authors and talk about both personal and professional issues.

Youthworker Update
1-800-769-7624
The *Update* offers up-to-the-minute information on the youth culture, trends, and ministry to teens. The newsletter format makes it easy to read and a quick resource.

CRISIS RESOURCES

The numbers and addresses listed below are just a few of the various agencies and services provided to meet needs that may arise in your ministry. Most of these groups can send you written information as well as offer a source of networking in a crisis situation. The list is by topic for easy referral. Please note the yellow pages of your local phone book for many local agencies and helpful services.

ABSTINENCE

Josh McDowell Ministries
West 22 Mission
Spokane, Washington 99201-2320
1-800-222-JOSH

National Institute of Youth Ministries
940 Calle Amanzcar, #G
San Clemente, California 92672
1-714-498-4418

AIDS

National AIDS Hotline (English)
1-800-342-2437

National AIDS Hotline (Spanish)
1-800-344-7432

National AIDS Hotline (Deaf)
1-800-243-7889

National AIDS Information Clearinghouse
P. O. Box 6003
Rockville, Maryland 20850
1-800-458-5231

CHEMICAL AND SUBSTANCE ABUSE

American Council for Drug Education
204 Monroe Street, Suite 110
Rockville, Maryland 20850
1-800-488-DRUG

National Clearinghouse for Alcohol and Drug Information
P.O. Box 2345
Rockville, Maryland 20847-2345
1-800-729-6686

Office on Smoking and Health Centers for Disease Control
Mail Stop K-50
4770 Buford Highway, N.E.
Atlanta, GA 30341-3724
1-404-488-5708

National Council on Alcoholism and Drug Dependence
12 West 21st Street
New York, New York 10010
1-800-622-2255

Center for Substance Abuse Treatment
Referral Hotline
1-800-662-HELP

CHILD ABUSE

National Center for Missing and Exploited Children
1-800-843-5678

Child Abuse Hotline
1-800-352-0386

COUNSELING NEEDS

Life Enrichment
14581 East Tufts Ave.
Aurora, CO 80015
1-303-693-3954
The counseling team offers biblical counseling for Christian leaders and their families. Counsel is available by phone, during extended stays in Colorado (three days to two weeks), or on-site when consulting with churches and non-profit ministries.

New Life Treatment Center
570 Glennyre, Suite 107
Laguna Beach, California 92651
1-800-NEW-LIFE
New Life Treatment Centers offer a wide range of counseling services, dealing with a variety of crisis situations including eating disorders, sexual abuse, substance abuse, and depression. They may be able to help you find a Christian resource in your area through their large network of counselors.

Pine Rest Christian Mental Health Services
300 68th St. South East
Grand Rapids, MI 49501
1-800-678-5500
Christian psychiatric care is offered with a special sensitivity to clergy and their family members. Outpatient counseling services are also available in the selected cities.

CRISIS PREGNANCY

For information about what help might be available, you should definitely check with local agencies. If you are still uncertain about the help that is available, contact the Christian Action Council at 1-703-478-5661 between the hours of 9:00 A.M. and 5:30 P.M. eastern time. They should be able to help you find a contact in your area.

RAPE
National Rape Hotline
1-800-222-7273

RUNAWAYS

Runaway Hotline
Austin, Texas
1-800-231-6946

National Runaway Switchboard
1-800-621-4000

TEEN MOTHERS

Teen Mother Choices
1-708-680-9345
TMC is a Chicago suburban ministry reaching teens that choose to parent their children. They mentor, teach parenting skills, and provide baby-sitting programs with the hope that the teens will develop skills to help them become self-sufficient, while exposing them to the life-changing power of Jesus Christ.

Home Family Care Network
6617 S. Laflin St.
Chicago, IL 60636
1-312-925-5999
Located in the heart of Chicago, HFCN shares the love of Christ with the young women and future mothers in their community. Programs include: mentoring, child-birth classes, and single-parent workshops.

OTHER RESOURCES

Focus on the Family Resource Lists:
Correspondence Department
Colorado Springs, CO 80995
1-719-531-5181
Focus on the Family will provide free five to ten page information sheets on the following ministry topics: "Teens" (MS109), "Parents and Youth Workers" (MS101), "Troubled Teens" (FX214), "Reaching Out to Youth" (FX066), and "Youth Ministry — The Challenge of Reaching Youth in the '90s" (FX331). Information includes books, tapes, videos, and conference listings.

AUDIO CASSETTE TAPES

Journey Publications
P.O. Box 594
Lincolnshire, IL 60069
Write for a complete listing. The tapes are from the Journey conferences including topics such as: "Appointment for Disappointment" by Helen Musick, "Women of Destiny" by Nancy Wilson, "Finishing Well" by Lynn Ziegenfuss, "Help, I'm Pregnant" by Christa March, and the teachings of the **"Breaking the Gender Barrier in Youth Ministry" conference tapes that coincide with this book.**

Moody Broadcasting Network
820 N. LaSalle Blvd.
Chicago, IL 60610
1-312-329-8010
Write and request the Cassette Ministry Full Line Catalog Expanded Edition for the current year.